# MINDFULNESS AND MEDITATION

## HANDLING LIFE WITH A CALM AND FOCUSED MIND

WHITNEY STEWART

TWENTY-FIRST CENTURY BOOKS™ / MINNEAPOLIS

To my niece Maggie Stewart, for her wisdom and courage

I extend my gratitude to my teachers and mindful friends whose wisdom and kindness helped me to become a happier and more balanced person. In particular, I would like to thank His Holiness the Dalai Lama, Venerable Khenchen Gyaltsen, Venerable Drupon Samten, Geshe Rinchen Choegyal, Fleet Maull, Kate Crisp, Gina Biegel, and Helen Maffini. Thanks also to Elizabeth Kahn, Judi Holst, Sally Rippin, Dominic Caputo, Marni Becker-Avin, Adam Avin, and all the teens I interviewed—many of whom asked me to change their names for privacy—and to my husband and son, Hans and Christoph Andersson, for their enduring support. To the readers of this book, I dedicate the merit of mindfulness to you.

Text copyright © 2020 by Whitney Stewart

Twenty-First Century Books™
An imprint of Lerner Publishing Group, Inc.
241 First Avenue North
Minneapolis, MN 55401 USA

For reading levels and more information, look up this title at www.lernerbooks.com.

Main body text set in Adobe Garamond Pro Regular.
Typeface provided by Adobe Systems.

**Library of Congress Cataloging-in-Publication Data**

Names: Stewart, Whitney, 1959– author.
Title: Mindfulness and meditation : handling life with a calm and focused mind / Whitney Stewart.
Description: Minneapolis, MN : Twenty-First Century Books, [2019] | Audience: Age: 14–18. | Audience: Grade 9 to 12. | Includes bibliographical references and index.
Identifiers: LCCN 2018038797 (print) | LCCN 2018053737 (ebook) | ISBN 9781541562707 (eb pdf) | ISBN 9781541540217 (lb : alk. paper)
Subjects: LCSH: Stress management for teenagers—Juvenile literature. | Mindfulness (Psychology)—Juvenile literature. | Meditation—Juvenile literature.
Classification: LCC BF724.3.S86 (ebook) | LCC BF724.3.S86 S74 2019 (print) | DDC 155.5/182—dc23

LC record available at https://lccn.loc.gov/2018038797

Manufactured in the United States of America
2-51378-36608-11/16/2021

# CONTENTS

# WHEN LIFE CAME CRASHING DOWN

I started high school confident, athletic, and intellectually curious. When I wasn't tossing a ball or rock climbing, I tried out for plays or studied. I was motivated and college-bound. My school asked me to speak at an alumni day. So, as a freshman, I stood before adults and spoke about individualism. I thought I was wise and could handle anything.

I was wrong.

In tenth grade, I had knee trouble and couldn't keep up on varsity lacrosse team runs. I went to a surgeon, who told me that if I quit competitive sports, I would still be walking at the age of forty. If not, I'd probably be in a wheelchair. I didn't think I had much of a choice, so I quit. After that, my field hockey and lacrosse coach, who had paid so much attention to me as a promising freshman, ignored me. My teammates were busy with practice, so I also lost my pack of friends. Instead of seeing myself as strong and dynamic, and using my energy in hard workouts, I sat around and felt like a quitter. The more I imagined myself that way, the weaker I became. I stopped eating well and spent time studying alone and feeling stressed out. My mind was always racing, and I couldn't sleep. I didn't know whom to talk to or how to admit my troubling thoughts and feelings.

Adding to my stress was family turbulence. Several family members battled alcoholism or drug addiction, and I was sexually assaulted and didn't know how to talk about it. I was ashamed to tell anyone and afraid of the consequences of doing so. Life felt like one long string of crises, and I was always on guard, expecting the worst.

Then I saw a sign for a yoga class. Back then, in the 1970s, many people thought yoga was weird or radical, but I decided to try it. I immediately loved this form of moving meditation; it helped me feel inner peace, at least some of the time. I was sixteen and my life started to shift—ever so slowly. I don't mean that a few yoga classes took away my problems. They didn't—not by a long shot. Chaos at home continued. Pressure to do well in school continued. And I was hard on myself.

As a young writer in the 1980s, I spent time in Asia and learned how to meditate. Back home, I began to meditate regularly and learned to sit more comfortably with my difficult emotions. Through this practice, I began to question my negative thoughts and to accept things I couldn't control. I gradually learned to relax more and to trust change and uncertainty.

But my story is only one of many. We all need ways to deal with our emotions and challenges. Sometimes that feels impossible. I wrote this book as a guide to finding a way to inner balance. We may not be able to change other people or circumstances, but we can change ourselves. If you're ready to work with your mind—and heart—mindfulness can get you started.

# 1
# MIND TRAINING:
# PRACTICE AND MORE PRACTICE

Matthieu Ricard doesn't call himself the "happiest man in the world," but many other people do. "It's absurd," he says of his nickname, explaining that he knows happier people. "I don't see everything as rosy," Ricard says, "but the ups and downs of life don't unsettle me in the usual way." Ricard, who was born in France, holds a PhD in molecular genetics. But he gave up his scientific career. Instead, he studied Buddhism, an ancient Asian religion, and became a Buddhist monk, a writer, and a photographer. Ricard lives in Nepal, where he runs an organization that provides health care, education, and social services to poor children. He also practices and writes about meditation, a mental discipline of staying focused and alert and resting the mind in a calm, relaxed, and natural state of awareness.

Studies reveal that people who meditate every day display increased activity in parts of the brain associated with happiness, focus, and memory.

In 2008 Ricard collaborated with Richard Davidson, a professor of psychology and psychiatry at the University of Wisconsin–Madison and director of the university's Center for Healthy Minds. Ricard allowed Davidson to attach 256 sensors to his scalp. Then, using an instrument called an electroencephalograph, Davidson measured the electrical impulses in Ricard's brain while he meditated. Davidson also scanned Ricard's brain during meditation using a technology called functional magnetic resonance imaging.

These analyses revealed that when Ricard focused his mind in meditation, the level of gamma waves in his brain were off the charts—no scientists had ever recorded such high levels. Gamma waves, the fastest of all brain waves, are linked to focus, information processing, and memory. During meditation, Ricard also demonstrated high levels of activity in his left prefrontal cortex, an area of the brain that's linked to happiness. The study provided evidence that meditation affects the brain in positive ways.

After testing Ricard, Davidson recruited twenty-one other Buddhist monks—all of them long-term practitioners of meditation—to participate in the same study. Their tests also revealed very high levels of focus and positivity, not just when they meditated but before and after meditation. The results showed that with meditation, the monks had trained their brains so well that the positive effects were enduring. Davidson and his research team reported his work in the journal *Proceedings of the National Academy of Sciences,* noting, "Practitioners understand 'meditation,' or mental training, to be a process of familiarization with one's own mental life leading to long-lasting changes in cognition [thinking] and emotion."

"The more you meditate, the stronger the lasting traits become. . . . We see it in cognitive changes. We see it in behavioral changes. And most importantly, we see it in neurological changes. . . . Right from the beginning [of meditation practice] there are attentional benefits. There are stress benefits. You're more resilient under stress."

—*Daniel Goleman, psychologist and science journalist*

Davidson and Daniel Goleman, a psychologist at Rutgers University in New Jersey, have written about this and similar studies in *Altered Traits: Science Reveals How Meditation Changes Your Mind, Brain, and Body.* Not all study subjects have been monks with years of meditation. Some studies have shown positive effects on the brains of new meditators—those with only eight weeks of daily mediation. Based on these studies, Ricard believes that anyone can train their brain for greater happiness. "If you can learn how to ride a bike, you can learn how to be happy," he says.

# ANCIENT ROOTS

Meditation is important in mindfulness. This practice can help you focus your mind, expand your awareness, understand your emotions, and become more at ease with life.

Mindfulness has its roots in ancient Buddhist teachings. The founder of Buddhism, Siddhartha Gautama, is called the historical Buddha, or the Buddha. He was born a prince in what is now Lumbini, Nepal, near the border with India, around 563 BCE. Although he lived in luxury, he witnessed human suffering—such as sickness and pain—outside his palace walls. He was inspired to abandon his princely life and seek a way to transcend suffering. Siddhartha tried severe self-punishments, such as denying himself food, but this only left him weakened. Eventually, Siddhartha simply meditated under a tree. There he achieved enlightenment—a state of mental and spiritual awareness, free from disturbing emotions. For the rest of his life, he taught others how to train their minds and achieve enlightenment.

Meditation has its roots in Buddhism, an ancient religion of Asia. Siddhartha Gautama, shown here in a meditation pose, founded the religion around 500 BCE. This ink-and-watercolor illustration was made in Tibet between 1450 and 1600 CE.

The Buddha's teachings evolved into the Buddhist religion. It spread throughout India and then to China, Korea, Japan, and other places in Asia. For several thousand years after the Buddha's death, people practiced Buddhism only in Asia. People in other parts of the world followed different religious traditions. But in the nineteenth and twentieth centuries, some Westerners began to study the Buddha's teachings. In the 1960s, great cultural and social change occurred in the United States. Black Americans and their allies fought for their civil rights, women fought for equality with men, and young people protested against US involvement in the Vietnam War (1957–1975). Many young Americans also questioned the religious, economic, and political values of their parents. They wanted to explore new lifestyles and spiritual paths. Some young people traveled to India, Nepal, Burma, Thailand, and Japan to study with Buddhist teachers. Some tried meditation. Others learned yoga, a traditional practice of meditation, physical postures, breathing techniques, and ethical discipline rooted in Hinduism, another religion of India.

In the 1970s, several Americans who had studied Buddhism, meditation, and yoga in Asia decided to teach the practices when they returned to the United States. For example, after working in the Peace Corps (a US government overseas service program) in Thailand, Jack Kornfield trained as a Buddhist monk in Thailand, India, and Burma. He returned home and in 1975, with two friends—Sharon Salzberg, who had studied meditation in India, and Joseph Goldstein, who had also served in the Peace Corps in Thailand—founded the Insight Meditation Society in Barre, Massachusetts. These three teachers went on to open other centers and introduced many Americans to mindfulness.

Jon Kabat-Zinn became interested in meditation in the 1960s when he was studying molecular biology at the Massachusetts Institute of Technology in Cambridge, Massachusetts. He began a regular meditation practice at the Cambridge Zen Center. (Zen is a Japanese

In the 1970s, Professor Jon Kabat-Zinn developed a program called mindfulness-based stress reduction. His studies have shown that mindfulness can lower anxiety and help heal the body.

school of Buddhism.) Kabat-Zinn's academic research focused on using the mind to help heal the body. As a professor at the University of Massachusetts Medical School, he developed a secular (nonreligious) mindfulness program for health. Called mindfulness-based stress reduction, the program combines meditation, body awareness, and yoga. During his medical career, Kabat-Zinn studied the positive effects of mindfulness-based stress reduction on people with stress-related disorders, chronic pain, and cancer. He also taught mindfulness to thousands, including business leaders, Olympic athletes, lawyers, religious leaders, students, and prison inmates. Kabat-Zinn also teamed with longtime friends Daniel Goleman and Richard Davidson to study how mindfulness positively effects the brain. Their work has helped to establish mindfulness programs in schools, health-care facilities, and workplaces.

Mindfulness practice has expanded since its introduction to Americans. With advances in technology come new medical tools, such as using an electroencephalograph and functional magnetic resonance imaging to study the brain waves of people when they meditate.

Researchers have also invented software to help meditators focus their minds and control their breath. For example, cell phone mindfulness and meditation apps such as Headspace, Calm, and Stop, Breathe, and Think encourage users to stare at a pulsing blue dot or at a nature image and breathe rhythmically—mind-training techniques based on centuries-old wisdom.

## EXPLORING MINDFULNESS FURTHER

Kabat-Zinn's work inspired a good working definition of mindfulness: paying attention, on purpose, with patience, to your inner and outer experiences, without judgment.

Let's look at that definition more precisely:

- Mindfulness is a way of *paying attention on purpose*. You're not on autopilot, doing things without noticing. Instead, you are *choosing* to experience your life with your full attention and open awareness.
- *With patience* means that you calmly and slowly train your mind to focus on what's happening in the present. Your mind might wander, but you patiently bring it back to attention.
- In mindfulness, you focus on *inner and outer experiences.* Inner experiences are your thoughts, emotions, and physical sensations. Outer experiences are those that happen around you, which you take in through your senses.
- You pay attention *without judgment*. This means you notice what is happening, but you let go of opinions about it. You focus on what you are seeing, hearing, tasting, touching, smelling, or sensing and not on what you are *thinking* about the experiences.

Mindfulness is about paying attention to what is happening *right now*—not what you remember happening nor what you anticipate will happen. While you are trying to focus, you might notice what some call "monkey mind." This endless chatter in the mind can take your attention away from what you are doing.

When you practice mindfulness and focus your attention, your monkey mind may quiet down. Then you might notice a relaxed awareness, which some call "wisdom mind." Then you are no longer mentally narrating your experience. You are simply living it. Being it.

Mindfulness meditation is a way of resting the mind in a calm and natural state of awareness. Meditators use many different techniques. Some meditators focus on their breathing or on a mental image and keep their bodies still while sitting or lying down. Other meditators walk slowly, with their attention on their feet or on what they take in through their senses. Most meditators practice every day, for as little as five minutes to an hour—or even more. Some people even go on occasional meditation retreats where they meditate for many hours per day.

As Davidson's study revealed, those who consistently practice mindfulness and meditation may experience positive effects on their mental health. The more you practice, the stronger and more lasting the benefits. These benefits can include

"Meditation is the only intentional, systematic human activity which at bottom is about not trying to improve yourself or get anywhere else, but simply to realize where you already are."

—*Jon Kabat-Zinn, scientist, author, and meditation teacher*

- increased awareness and concentration
- reacting less emotionally to difficult situations
- having more resilience, or recovering more quickly from a stressful event

- having reduced sensations of physical pain
- improved memory
- increased empathy and generosity

## WHAT MINDFULNESS *ISN'T*

You may have heard wild claims about mindfulness: *It's a cure-all! It will make you smarter, richer, and better looking!* This hype could give you the wrong idea. Often people make unproven or exaggerated claims about mindfulness. This is what mindfulness is not:

- Mindfulness is not just for those who are rich, beautiful, and famous. You may have seen magazine covers showing models in meditation poses. That's marketing. Mindfulness is for anyone, from any background and no matter how they look. You don't need lots of money, equipment, or specialized clothing to practice mindfulness. You only need a willingness to pay attention.
- Mindfulness is not a quick fix. It's mind training. Just as improving your physical fitness through gym workouts can take weeks or months, mindfulness also takes time and patience.
- Mindfulness is not all bliss. When you practice mindfulness, you might discover difficult thoughts and emotions you hadn't noticed or accepted before. This doesn't mean you're doing mindfulness *wrong*. With practice, you can learn to sit patiently with whatever you experience.
- Mindfulness is not a replacement for critical thinking about difficult problems to find reasonable solutions.

Instead, mindfulness can help you calm and focus your mind to prepare for and help you through critical thinking.

- Mindfulness is not prayer. In mindfulness, you're not asking a divine power outside of yourself to change you or your situation. You are witnessing the present moment of experience and training your mind to stay focused on it.
- Mindfulness is not a religion. The secular practice incorporates ancient mind-training methods. If you are religious, mindfulness can coexist with your beliefs.
- Mindfulness is not a replacement for medical or mental health treatment. Sitting still and focusing attention might *not* be helpful for people with certain medical conditions or illnesses. If you are suffering from depression or anxiety, mindfulness can be part of your plan to deal with it, but you should also talk to a trusted adult and seek professional help. If you have any doubts, check with your medical practitioner before you begin practicing mindfulness.

Mindfulness is also not a solution if you are being harassed or assaulted. Mindfulness might help you to stay calm and deal with trauma after a stressful event, but it doesn't replace seeking help. If you are in trouble, confide in a trusted adult or friend. Self-care, an important part of mindfulness, is knowing what you need to stay safe, healthy, and well. It is treating yourself with kindness and patience and taking positive actions to benefit yourself. Self-care is not the same as being selfish. It involves treating yourself with love and respect. So if you need to speak up to keep yourself safe, speak up!

# CROSS-SECTION OF THE HUMAN BRAIN, RIGHT HEMISPHERE

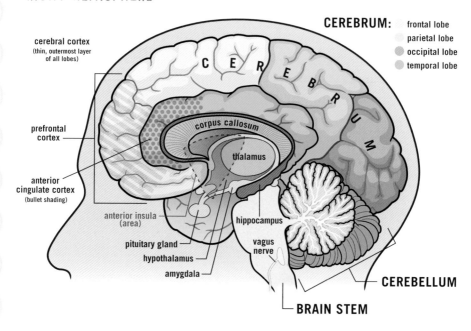

**CEREBRUM:**
- frontal lobe
- parietal lobe
- occipital lobe
- temporal lobe

cerebral cortex
(thin, outermost layer
of all lobes)

CEREBRUM

corpus callosum

thalamus

prefrontal
cortex

anterior
cingulate cortex
(bullet shading)

anterior insula
(area)

hippocampus

pituitary gland

vagus
nerve

hypothalamus

amygdala

CEREBELLUM

BRAIN STEM

Using electroencephalographs, functional magnetic resonance imaging, and other scanning technology, scientists can monitor how meditation affects specific areas of the brain. This diagram shows major brain structures.

## THE QUESTIONING MIND

Some people may think that sitting still for five, ten, or even twenty minutes a day doesn't sound as fun as going to a party, playing sports, or using your smartphone. Mindfulness is not exciting the way a giant waterslide is. But mindfulness can be interesting—even exciting—as a way of getting to know yourself. Having the ability to stay calm and focused under pressure or to feel content and resilient every day can take you far.

# 2
# GETTING STARTED:
# HOW DO I DO THIS?

If you want to try mindfulness, try the exercises in this chapter. You could do them in any order. There are no rules. Read through them, and decide if you want to try one, two, or all three of them.

These and the other exercises in this book are guided meditations—you follow a series of prompts, step by step, as you meditate. During group meditation, a teacher gives the prompts verbally. When you listen to a meditation app, you also hear spoken prompts. This book has written prompts. You could ask a friend to read them aloud to you as you meditate. Or you could read and record the prompts using your smartphone and play them back as you meditate. Or read the guiding words to yourself before you begin.

Sometimes the final step in a meditation exercise is sitting still. Or

You can meditate almost anywhere. Here, high school students sit on top of their school desks, while a teacher leads them in guided meditation.

you can focus on your breathing while you sit and for as long as you want with no firm stopping point. People often ask how long they should sit. Start with an amount of time you can manage—two or three minutes— and build from there. You might want to set a timer with a soft chime to go off after a certain number of minutes, to signal the end of your session. If you don't have a timer, you could ask a friend to tap you lightly on the shoulder or whisper to you to end your meditation. Or you can meditate until you feel you are ready to stop. There is no magic or right amount of time to meditate. As you get used to meditation, you could find yourself staying seated longer and longer, letting your mind settle. You can experiment and see what amount of time feels right.

You can meditate almost anywhere. Some people set up a meditation space in their home that feels inspirational, and they return to it daily. You may not have a place for regular meditation. That's okay. Find any place inside or outside where you'll be comfortable sitting still. Some people need a quiet place. Other people learn to focus their mind with noises around them. See what works for you.

Sitting in a meditation posture helps your mind and body relax and expands your awareness. The traditional way is to sit on a firm meditation cushion on the floor with your legs crossed, but you can also sit on a folded blanket. Rest your hands, palms down, on your thighs, or place your hands in your lap with your right hand, palm up, in your open left palm, thumbs touching. Or sit up straight in a chair with a firm back. Plant your feet firmly on the ground, and place your hands, palms down, on your thighs. Whichever way you choose, sit up tall but relax. An elongated spine allows your breath to move more easily through you and helps calm your monkey mind.

Some people like to meditate in a prone (lying-down) position. This posture might help you relax more deeply, especially if you are listening to a guided meditation. Lie on a blanket or mat on the floor, or lie on a couch or bed. Put a firm cushion, rolled towel, or yoga block under your head. You can also rest your head on a book with a sweater or towel for cushioning. Stretch out your legs. Touch your ankles together, and let your feet fall away from each other. Rest your arms by your sides. The challenge of meditating lying down is that you may fall asleep in this position. If so, it may be a sign that you needed a nap. After a good rest, try meditation again and see what happens. You might also fall asleep in a sitting meditation posture. To resist falling asleep in seated meditation, try keeping your eyes open and lifting your gaze higher to let in more light.

Before you begin to meditate, don't have a goal for your meditation. The benefits of mindfulness can include feeling calmer, more focused, or less anxious. But having a goal for a mindfulness session can sometimes be a setup for frustration. For example, if you are meditating and your goal is to feel calm, you might spend your session waiting for that calm state of mind to take hold. If it doesn't, you might think you are doing something wrong or that you are failing at meditation. Goals are about the future. They prevent us from paying attention to the present and accepting whatever happens. It's more helpful to have an intention in mindfulness practice. Your intention might be to stay open to and aware of your experiences. Or you could trust your wisdom mind and drop expectations. With intentions, you accept the present. You allow an experience to be what it is, without trying to shape or interpret it.

# MEDITATION POSTURE

Experienced meditators have found that posture matters. Proper posture can help you feel awake and alert, as well as relaxed. It also helps calm your busy mind. Most people meditate in a sitting position with an elongated spine. If that's your approach, follow these guidelines:

- Sit in a chair with your feet planted on the floor, or sit on a cushion or folded blanket on the floor with your legs crossed. Put a sticky mat under your blanket, or place your blanket on a rug or carpet so it doesn't shift.

- If you're meditating on the floor, sit on the forward edge of a firm cushion or folded blanket. This will help lift your buttocks slightly higher than your knees and will naturally tilt your pelvic bones forward and down. This helps your alignment and eases tension in your back and knees.

- Rest your hands, palms down, on your thighs, or place your hands in your lap with your right hand, palm up, resting in your open left palm, thumbs touching.

- Elongate your spine. Avoid slumping. Remain relaxed, not stiff.

- Let your shoulders drop and stay level.

- Tuck your chin in slightly, and relax your jaw.

- Touch the tip of your tongue to the back of your teeth to prevent excessive salivation and to help relax your jaw.

- Keep your eyes slightly open, and gaze down with unfocused eyes a few inches below your nose. (If keeping your eyes open is distracting, start with your eyes closed and open them after you feel more settled. Raise your gaze if you feel sleepy. Lower it if you are distracted.)

Most people meditate while seated on the floor. You can also sit in a chair or lie down. This infographic shows six traditional meditation postures.

Lotus

Half Lotus

Burmese

Chair

Seiza

Prone

# BREATH MEDITATION

Mindfulness usually begins with breath meditation. You use your breath as an anchor for your attention. Many of the meditations and exercises in this book have you take three mindful breaths to begin. You pay full attention as you take air into your nose and body for three inhales and then make three exhales. You can try it with this meditation:

## Simple Breath Meditation

Sit in a meditation posture, and start by taking three mindful breaths.

Notice the expansion and contraction of your chest and belly as you breathe.

Relax more and more with each breath.

Imagine sinking deeply into your seat.

After taking three mindful breaths, allow your attention to stay lightly on your breathing.

If it helps you focus, count each outbreath like this:

Breathe in normally, and then exhale and count one.

Breathe in again, exhale, and count two.

Continue breathing and counting each exhalation, up to ten.

Then count each exhalation, starting again at one.

When your mind can stay focused on your breathing, let go of the counting.

Notice the slight natural gap or pause at the end of each outbreath before you breathe in again.

Relax your muscles with each pause in your breathing.

If you start thinking of something, bring your mind back to the pause between your outbreath and your next inbreath.

Relax and breathe.

If you lose focus, return to counting your exhalations.

Continue this pattern until you feel ready to stop or when your alarm chimes.

# WHAT'S HAPPENING IN YOUR MIND?

How did this meditation go for you? Could you focus your mind on your breathing? What did you feel during the pause between breaths? If this is the first time you've meditated, probably you noticed your breathing for a little while and then became distracted by a thought or a flood of thoughts. Our thoughts are usually about something that happened in the past—a memory—or about something that will happen—a worry or anticipation. Sometimes our thoughts turn toward something we hear or feel in our physical environment, such as a loud noise or people talking in another room. Thoughts take us out of the present. Then we miss the deeper experience of awareness.

Let's say you sit down to meditate, but the minute you are quiet, you think about the concert you went to last night. You had a great time, and you replay scenes from the evening in your head. You still feel the excitement of the night, and your body tenses or wiggles. Maybe you hear the lyrics of your favorite song, which brings up emotions. Before you know it, you've forgotten to pay attention to your breathing. Breath? What breath?

Dhyana mudra

This traditional hand posture is called the Dhyana mudra. The name means "meditation gesture" in Sanskrit, an ancient language of India.

Or maybe your thoughts during meditation aren't happy. Maybe you've had an argument with a friend and you're going over it in your head. Just thinking about the argument triggers physical responses, such as a fast heartbeat, a headache, or stomachache. Perhaps sitting still, doing nothing, makes you feel as if you will obsess about this bad experience, and you can't stand the physical sensations in your body.

Or you might start thinking about the meditation itself. For example, you may experience mental commentary about what you are doing. "Is this meditation? Am I doing it right? I'm just breathing. Is something else supposed to happen? My knees hurt. I wonder how much time has gone by. This is boring." These thoughts are common. Just notice them and return to focusing on your breath.

Sometimes external noises or smells distract us. We might think we want to stop meditating and investigate the noise or smell instead. Or you might feel an itch and want to scratch it. Those are great times to notice how easy it is to become distracted. Notice the sensation of the itch without scratching it right away, or notice the quality of the sound or smell without investigating it. Notice what your mind starts telling you about the itch, the sound, or the smell. When any of these things happen, remember that distraction is a normal part of meditation and of life.

Here's how to unravel what might be going on. The human mind thinks. Thoughts are natural. When you sit still and focus on your breath, you confront the inner workings of your mind. You might come to realize that your thoughts often control you. They hide beneath the surface, triggering you to feel or act a certain way.

When you meditate, thoughts will come front and center. That's common, and meditators learn to accept this experience with patience and to view thoughts with curiosity. Thoughts can be a doorway to a deeper meditation.

In this next exercise, you will speak your thoughts aloud in a soft voice. You may want to find a place to be alone so you can whisper everything that crosses your mind without worrying that others will overhear you. Or do this exercise with a group of friends, all whispering at the same time. The point of the exercise is to notice the extent of your mental chatter and to connect it to your awareness.

## Voicing Your Thoughts

Sit in a meditation posture, and start by taking three mindful breaths.
Notice the expansion and contraction of your chest and belly as you breathe.
Relax more and more with each breath.
Imagine sinking deeply into your seat.

When you feel more settled, notice your thinking.
Turn your attention to your specific thoughts.
Whisper aloud every thought that comes into your mind.
Keep whispering until you run out of thoughts or exhaust yourself with the chatter.

Nothing else needs to happen.
You are breathing and voicing your thoughts.
When you stop whispering thoughts, sit in stillness.
End your meditation when you feel ready or when your alarm chimes.

# YOU ARE MORE THAN YOUR THOUGHTS

Did voicing your thoughts feel silly? The first time I tried it, I couldn't believe how fast my thoughts kept coming. I have a very busy mind. As soon as I stopped voicing thoughts, I appreciated the silence.

One meditation teacher compared meditation to "slipping into a warm bath." You step in, sink into the water, relax, and let out a big sigh: "Aah!" That's a soothing image of meditation, but your actual practice may not fit that image. Sometimes meditation sessions are more like a rodeo. You may be swinging a lasso, trying to wrangle

## THREE MINDFUL BREATHS

Many of the meditation exercises in this book start with the phrase "Take three mindful breaths." This prompt asks you to notice your breathing for three inhalations and exhalations.

You take three soft, slow breaths and feel them in your body. Notice the air coming into your nose as you breathe in. Notice it filling your lungs and expanding your chest and abdomen. Notice your breath again as you breathe out your nose or mouth. Notice the contraction in your chest and abdomen with each exhalation.

The point of three mindful breaths is to stay aware of and focused on your breathing. Some exercises ask you to continue to focus on your breath and body after the initial three mindful breaths. Focusing on your breathing helps you relax and become more aware of your surroundings and your inner life.

your thoughts. Other times, the session may start like an action movie showing on four screens at once. Slowly, you will settle down to watch the scenes in your mind. After a while, they may make you laugh. You might say to yourself, "There I go again, thinking, thinking, thinking."

When you watch your thoughts but don't identify with them, you might experience wisdom mind. Wisdom mind feels like an expansiveness and a connectedness to everything and everyone. This is hard to describe because no words really capture this knowing. It is an awareness beyond thinking.

# THE CONSTRUCTED SENSE OF SELF

To experience wisdom mind, it helps to let go of your constructed sense of self. What is this?

It is the idea of yourself that comes from defining who you are with social labels or mental attitudes. It's who you think you're supposed to be. Your constructed sense of self might include labels like student, athlete, artist, meditator, friend, or family member, plus all the concepts or expectations that you add to those labels. On hard days, your constructed sense of self might also include feelings of being unworthy, unqualified, or unattractive. Sometimes we're our harshest critics, and that feels awful.

Breaking away from your constructed sense of self is not easy—especially in this age of selfies and online profiles—but it can be liberating. This next meditation might help you break through a fixation on your constructed sense of self.

## VISUALIZING THE POSTURE

To keep your spine and body straight and still when you sit and meditate, it helps to create a picture of them in your mind. See if one of these visualizations works for you:

- A stack of coins. Imagine your spine as a stack of coins from your tailbone to the top of your head. Keep them aligned as you meditate.

- A mountain. Imagine your buttocks as the base of a mountain. Grounded on Earth, you extend skyward, strong and unmoving.

- Puppet string. Imagine you have a string attached to the top of your head that pulls you up tall. Your pelvic bones tilt forward slightly, which extends your spine.

stack of coins

mountain

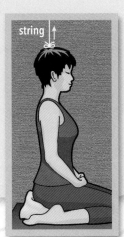

string

## Who Are You?

Sit in a meditation posture, and start by taking three mindful breaths.

Notice the expansion and contraction of your chest and belly as
    you breathe.

Relax more and more with each breath.

Imagine sinking deeply into your seat.

Turn your attention onto yourself.

See an image of who you are in your mind.

Imagine yourself as a jigsaw puzzle, with many pieces.

Each piece represents a label you give yourself or a judgment
    about yourself.

Think about how you came by those labels and judgments.

Did someone call you a name and it stuck?

Did you define yourself a certain way to fit into a group?

Did someone call out a strength that you are proud of?

What does it feel like to be a jigsaw puzzle of so many pieces?

Imagine the puzzle breaking apart and the pieces scattering.

Where are you now? Who are you now?

Breathe into the empty space where your pieces used to be.

Connect to it.

Rest there for a while, breathing quietly.

You have the choice to put your puzzle pieces back together or to remain
    in that openness.

Do you want to keep some of the pieces and let others go?

You can choose now.

Give yourself time.

When you are ready, shift your attention back to the physical sensations
    in your body.

Notice the way your buttocks contact the surface below you.

Notice how you are holding your hands. Are they tense or relaxed? Are they open or closed?

Notice your jaw muscles. What do they feel like?

Take in another deep breath, and relax all of your muscles.

End your meditation when you are ready or when your timer goes off.

# FINDING YOU UNDER THE PUZZLE PIECES

Meditating on your self-image can show the underlying thoughts you might have about yourself during the day. We often fixate on small aspects of ourselves that we like or don't like, sometimes without knowing it. If anyone challenges the image we want to project—of being a smart and confident person, for example—we might get angry or defensive. Or we might feel crushed and grow silent. We wonder why people don't see us the way we want to be seen. We expend a great deal of mental energy trying to prove something to ourselves or others.

Focusing on ourselves can carry us away, even when we want to be present for someone else. For instance, have you ever been listening to a friend tell a story and find your mind wandering onto something about yourself? Before you know it, you realize you haven't heard a word your friend said because you were caught up in your own thoughts. Or maybe you were just waiting for the chance to tell your story, because it felt so important.

Self-directed thinking (focusing on yourself) is not a bad thing. If we never paid attention to ourselves, we might not realize when we're hungry and need food or when we're tired and need sleep. Without self-reflection, we might not discover what we value or what gives us a sense of purpose. Self-directed thinking can be a great tool for uncovering deeper wisdom. It's that deeper wisdom—awareness beyond thinking—that is our true strength.

# 3
# BUSY MIND!
# WORKING WITH THOUGHTS

Your experiences are channeled through your mind. Your eyes see something, your ears hear something, or your fingers touch something. The concepts in our minds help us identify and name what we are seeing, hearing, or touching. All those mental concepts come from what you have learned—the language you speak, the attitudes you've adopted, and the experiences you've had.

For example, if you have a friendly and supportive teacher at school, you may develop positive ideas about teachers in general. If, however, you have a teacher who goes around the room singling out students and humiliating them when they do not immediately understand a difficult concept, you might have a negative view of teachers. You might think you are ignorant and dread going to class. Or you might feel challenged and determined to prove your teacher wrong.

Our everyday experiences help shape our thoughts. You can use mindfulness to better understand your thoughts and to reframe negative ones.

The stories in your mind fuel your emotions and often determine your actions. Sometimes these stories are so powerful that they inspire you to do great things. Other times, they are full of conflict and bring on negative emotions. Imagine that a hurricane is approaching, and you are unable to leave town ahead of the storm. You are trapped at home and afraid. Suppose the storm knocks out the electric power, and your home floods. You may see yourself as a victim as you focus on your difficult situation. If you have trouble moving beyond seeing yourself as a victim, even after the storm is over, your emotional hardship is likely to intensify. Professionals call this common response to trauma post-traumatic stress disorder. With this disorder, you might feel anxiety when a new storm is forecast or the winds pick up. To deal with trauma, many experts suggest changing the story line in your mind. For example, a person who has lived through a devastating hurricane can shift from that of a victim to someone who is lucky to have survived the storm. Experts also point out that people who help in a disaster are more able to manage negative emotions and post-traumatic stress disorder. For example, volunteering to help clean up storm damage, helping neighbors clean up their homes, or raising money for families left homeless by the storm could shift your emotions away from your own suffering and help you feel empowered.

The following exercises can help you examine your thoughts and work with the stories in your mind. Experiment to see which ones inspire you. The first exercise explores the challenge of stopping your thoughts. Choose the amount of time you wish for each exercise. You could start with three minutes and expand the time if that feels right.

## Stopping Your Thoughts

Sit in a meditation posture, and start by taking three mindful breaths.

Notice the expansion and contraction of your chest and belly as you breathe.

Relax more and more with each breath.

Imagine sinking deeply into your seat.

Notice your thoughts, and tell yourself to stop thinking.

Do whatever you can to silence your thoughts: hum, tap your fingers, or bounce your knees.

Distract yourself to silence your brain.

Keep it up until you have cleared your mind of thoughts or until you decide you aren't able to during this session.

End this exercise when you are ready.

How did it go? Were you able to stop your thoughts? If so, how did you do it? Would this technique work whenever you need it? What did you experience when you had no thoughts?

If you were unable to stop your thoughts, what happened in your mind? Did the same thoughts keep coming back? Or did different thoughts arrive? Reflect on the way your mind works.

People have a hard time stopping their thoughts by trying to force the mind to submit. The method backfires and triggers even more thinking. Did that happen to you? Mindfulness is not about trying to stop your thoughts. It's about being aware of them and sitting still with the experience. This next exercise shifts the mind to watching thoughts:

## Watching Your Thoughts

Sit in a meditation posture, and start by taking three mindful breaths.
Notice the expansion and contraction of your chest and belly as you
  breathe.
Relax more and more with each breath.
Imagine sinking deeply into your seat.

Notice the thoughts in your mind.
Imagine them as a giant fountain of multicolored water.
Your thoughts spurt upward into the sky.

Let yourself relax and watch the beautiful water fountain.
Just sit there, without focusing on or reacting to any particular thought.
Do you notice a pause between your thoughts?
End this exercise when you are ready.

What happened for you? Was your experience of the first exercise
different from that of the second? If so, in what ways?

In the first exercise, you tried to stop thoughts. In the second, you
watched thoughts from your observer mind, your wisdom mind. The
second exercise shows that your thoughts are not the essence of you
because something deeper can watch them. When you watch thoughts
without reacting to them, you help prevent them from controlling or
defining you.

"The moment you start watching the thinker [your thoughts], a higher level of
consciousness becomes activated. You then begin to realize that there is a vast realm
of intelligence beyond thought, that thought is only a tiny aspect of that intelligence.
You also realize that all the things that truly matter–beauty, love, creativity, joy, inner
peace–arise from beyond the mind. You begin to awaken."

—Eckhart Tolle, spiritual teacher and author

A third way to work with thoughts is to embrace them and explore the message they tell you.

## Probing Your Thoughts

Sit in a meditation posture, and start by taking three mindful breaths.
Notice the expansion and contraction of your chest and belly as
    you breathe.
Relax more and more with each breath.
Imagine sinking deeply into your seat.

Keep breathing mindfully.
Ask yourself, "How am I doing right now?"
Notice how your answer comes to you.
Is it a thought or a physical sensation?
Explore whatever comes.

If you have a worry, dig into it for understanding.
Ask yourself: Why did this worry come up now?
Is there a deeper message with this worry?
Give it your full attention.

If a strong physical sensation comes up with a thought, explore that too.
Is it a pleasant or unpleasant sensation?
Give it your full attention.

If a strong memory comes to your mind, explore it.
Why did this memory come now?
Sit with the answers or feelings that come.

Before you end your meditation, take three more deep mindful breaths.
Feel how they anchor you in your body.
End your meditation when you're ready.

The purpose of this exercise is to give your thoughts full attention until they loosen their grip on you. Sometimes when you deny your thoughts or ignore them, they simply scream more loudly until you say, "Okay. What do you want?" By giving them your attention, you can see if something important arises and then acknowledge whatever you've been ignoring.

Another way to work with thoughts is to label them without going deeply into them. This technique is useful when exploring thoughts that are painful and emotionally charged.

## Labeling Your Thoughts

Sit in a meditation posture, and start by taking three mindful breaths.
Notice the expansion and contraction of your chest and belly as
 you breathe.
Relax more and more with each breath.
Imagine sinking deeply into your seat.

Continue taking mindful breaths.
This time, with each inhalation, silently say to yourself, "Breathing in."
With each exhalation, silently say, "Breathing out."

If you become distracted by a thought, silently label the type of thought.
If your thought is irritating, say, "Irritating thought."
If your thought is sad, say, "Sad thought."
If your thought is happy, say, "Happy thought."
Then return to labeling your breaths: "Breathing in" and "Breathing out."

Continue labeling breaths or thoughts through the rest of this
 exercise session.
End your meditation when you are ready.

## LOCK THOUGHTS AWAY

If you want—or need—to put bothersome thoughts aside, try this visualization experiment. Let's say you want to go to sleep, but a dark thought is bothering you. Close your eyes and imagine putting the thought into a cupboard and locking it in there with a key. Take the key and hang it on a hook, in a safe place. Your thought is securely stored away for the night, and you can sleep free from its power. In the morning, you can decide what to do with the key and the thought. Maybe you will choose to take the key off the hook, unlock the cupboard, and take out the thought to reexamine it. Or you may choose to discard it. Or you may choose to leave it in the cupboard until another day—or forever.

If doing this in your mind isn't enough, write down the thought on a piece of paper and store it in a box, such as an old shoebox. You could call this your Thought Box. Feed your Thought Box with thoughts that bother you. You can take them out whenever you wish to reexamine them. Or you can throw them away if you decide you don't want them.

By labeling your breaths and thoughts, you can begin to see that both breathing and thinking are automatic and continual. As long as you are healthy and alive, you will breathe. As long as you are healthy and alive, your mind will think—although you might experience silent spaces between thoughts. By labeling your thoughts, you recognize them to be as freely flowing as your breath. They can come easily into your mind and flow out of your mind. You can also notice the quality of your thoughts. Do you tend to have more negative thoughts or positive thoughts?

Are you able to have a relaxed attitude toward thoughts when you meditate, letting them pass through you like your breath? Do thoughts come and go like clouds floating across the sky? Wisdom mind is that sky, unchanging no matter how many clouds pass across it.

# THE POWER OF DISBELIEVING

Another way to work with your critical or upsetting thoughts is to challenge the truth of them. Start with a thought that bothers you. Choose one that really gets under your skin. For example, "I'm not good enough" may be a thought that comes up when you are learning something new. Another might be, "I can't handle this."

The next guideline is important: Choose not to believe the thought. Don't accept it as truth, and don't try to suppress it. Simply notice the thought in your mind and challenge it.

## MAGGIE'S STORY

One teen, Maggie, had a persistent fearful thought before taking math tests. She kept telling herself she was not going to do well on tests, and she worried about getting a poor grade in class. She carried around a deep-seated dread, which often caused her to panic.

When she finally acknowledged her fears and went for help, her counselor encouraged her to examine her thoughts and her panic experiences deeply. Maggie began to question why she was not learning math skills as quickly as other students did. Slowly, she began to understand that she learned in a different way from her peers and needed math tutoring, which she got. And instead of repeatedly telling herself she would fail, she began to encourage herself mentally.

She went from earning C-minus grades in math at the beginning of the school year to earning A-minus grades by the end of the year. By looking at her thoughts and acknowledging something important she was ignoring, Maggie was able to change her own story about math and improve her grades.

Many people struggle with negative thoughts about their identity and looks and what others think of them. Through mindfulness meditation, you can reframe negative feelings and embrace positive self-love.

## Challenging Your Thoughts

Sit in a meditation posture, and start by taking three mindful breaths.

Notice the expansion and contraction of your chest and belly as you breathe.

Relax more and more with each breath.

Imagine sinking deeply into your seat.

Bring to mind the negative thought or phrase you keep hearing in your head.

Repeat it to yourself silently or out loud.

Notice how this thought makes you feel.

What physical sensations arise with this thought?

Does it make you feel sick to your stomach or dizzy?

Does it cause your heart to race or your muscles to tighten?
Just notice.

You are safe because this thought is only made of words in your mind.
This thought has no substance.

Actively tell yourself, "This thought is not true."
Repeat to yourself, "I do not believe this thought. It is not true."
It might have come from a story that you told yourself or that someone told you.
Ask yourself where this thought came from.
Why did you choose to believe it?

Ask yourself if you're holding onto this thought for some deep reason?
What would change if you didn't believe this thought?
Even if you think the thought was once true, let go of it.

Let it go with a deep exhalation, breathing out through your mouth.
Relax all your muscles when you let go of the thought.
Finally, replace this negative thought with a more helpful thought.
Repeat your new thought to yourself silently or out loud.
How does this new thought make you feel? Can you believe it?
What is different if you accept the new thought?

As you end this exercise, remind yourself: You are not your thoughts. And you can always change your mind.

Another way to challenge troublesome thoughts and replace them is through writing exercises. You can strengthen this process by continuing to identify and replace negative thoughts during the day.

## Challenging and Replacing Negative Thoughts

Write down answers to these questions:

- What is the negative thought I am having?
- How does it make me feel?
- Why does it make me feel this way?
- Do I have to allow it to make me feel this way?
- Why is holding onto this thought important to me?
- Could I talk about my negative thoughts with someone I trust?
- Could I watch this negative thought without feeling upset by it?
- Is it possible that my negative thought is not true?
- What would change if I did not believe this thought?
- Could I replace this thought with a positive thought?
- What is different if I believe the positive thought instead of the negative thought?

## WHEN THOUGHTS ARE TOO POWERFUL

Sometimes negative thoughts might be too powerful and persistent, and focusing on them is not helpful. Mindfulness can help you deal with them. But if you feel overwhelmed with depressing thoughts or thoughts about self-harm, seek professional help. Just practicing mindfulness on your own won't necessarily solve the problem.

Below are some examples of reframing negative thoughts. You can add other examples to the list.

| Negative Thoughts | Positive Thoughts |
|---|---|
| I don't look as good as . . . | There's only one me—I am unique. |
| I am anxious about this. | I am in charge of my emotions. |
| People think I'm weird. | I am comfortable being myself. |
| I failed. | I learn from my mistakes. |
| This is too hard. | I thrive on challenges. |
| I will never understand this. | I can ask someone for help. |
| I am really frightened. | I am brave and can handle challenge. |
| I hate those people. | I could get to know people I don't understand. |

Everyone has powerful thoughts. Sometimes those thoughts can trigger emotions that either inspire you or bring you down. You can get a handle on your thoughts through regular mindfulness practice. If, however, you believe your negative thinking is too much to handle, talk to someone you trust and ask for help.

# 4
# TICKED OFF!
## DEALING WITH EMOTIONS

Imagine you are walking down a hallway at school and someone insults your hair or your clothes. Other people stare at you and start laughing. You blush. Your muscles tense up, and you feel like throwing up. You feel so bad that you freeze up, go speechless, and slink away. You feel ashamed. Or maybe you get angry and scream or hit something. Perhaps a teacher comes along and scolds you for yelling. You feel hurt and furious about a second injustice.

Has something like that happened to you? How did you handle it? Did you become emotional? Maybe later you wished that you'd confronted the person who insulted you. Or maybe you wished that you'd walked away confidently, without worrying about what other people thought of or said about you. By bringing mindfulness to that kind of situation, you can take charge of your emotions and your reactions.

Lisa Feldman Barrett is a neuroscientist and psychologist at Northeastern University in Boston, Massachusetts. Her studies show that our brains construct our emotions. "Emotions that seem to happen to you are actually made by you," she says. For instance, if you felt tense and froze up in the school hallway and your face flushed, your mind might have interpreted your physical sensations as shame or anger. Imagine the situation again. Someone insults you and you tense up, freeze, and blush. This time, you say to yourself, "Wow! My body really reacted when someone mocked me. And I felt really hurt. Instead of running away or lashing out, I can meditate on these sensations and this emotion."

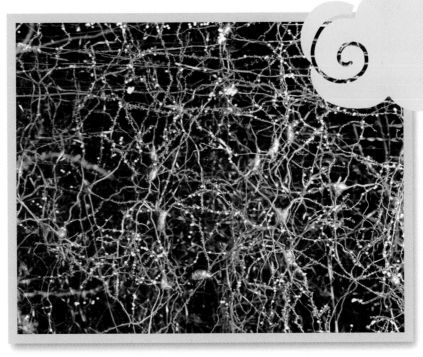

This computer-generated image shows countless neurons, or nerve cells, connected to one another in a network inside the human brain. Our experiences reinforce neural connections, creating our thoughts, attitudes, emotions, and beliefs.

# RESOLVING CONFLICT WITH MINDFULNESS

Most people tend to see the world through their own lens, and much suffering comes from obsessing about oneself. So it's hard to break away from our biases because they come from experiencing life through our senses, filtered through our own thoughts and emotions, which have been shaped by our unique experiences.

Many of us rarely take the time or think to ask people who are not family or close friends about their experiences. What if we could walk in someone else's shoes for a moment, live in their home, talk to their family members, and experience their challenges?

Without a broader view, we often encounter conflict when whatever *I* want clashes with what *you* want. We can reduce conflict by listening mindfully to each other without expectation and judgment. This helps when we're having trouble understanding another person's point of view or actions. Here are ten mindfulness steps for resolving conflict:

1. **Pause.** When a conflict arises, avoid lashing out. Take a moment to breathe slowly. Notice the air coming into and going out of your lungs and belly. Focusing on your breath can help ground you.

2. **Find the gap.** As you breathe, find the gap at the end of each outbreath before you breathe in again. Relax during this pause. Keep doing this for a few minutes, relaxing deeper and deeper with each gap between breaths.

3. **Scan your body.** Notice the physical sensations that you are experiencing. Are you tightening your fists, ready to hit something? Are your leg muscles twitching, urging you to flee? Are you clenching your jaws in anger or frustration? Notice any muscle tension, from your toes to the top of your head. Breathe deeply, let go, and relax your tight muscles. You could imagine sending warm light to any part of you that feels tense.

4. **Acknowledge your inner experiences.** Pay attention to your thoughts and emotions. Is your mind racing with angry thoughts? Do you feel hurt or embarrassed? Notice whatever you are experiencing. Remember, paying attention to thoughts and emotions without reacting to them is an effective way to help them settle calmly.

5. **Be patient.** Sometimes you may choose to accept that you are upset and not fight it. Your emotions might feel too strong to investigate. It's okay to acknowledge this reality to yourself and others. Move away from the troubling situation. You can choose to politely leave the room. Or you can let the other person know that you want to drop the conversation and return to the issue at another time when you are calmer.

6. **Avoid negative speech.** Name-calling is never helpful. Instead, explain your point of view clearly and in respectful language. Acknowledge the viewpoints of others even if you don't agree.

7. **Challenge your assumptions.** Don't assume you are right and the other person is wrong. Remember that you may not know what they are thinking or feeling. You may not understand all the circumstances that affect the situation. Ask open-ended questions so that you can truly understand their perspective. Explain your perspective without anger.

8. **Find a resolution.** Stick to the issue that is creating conflict. Avoid piling on other concerns or problems. Suggest one or more ways to resolve the conflict. Listen to the resolutions that other people suggest. Calmly discuss the pros and cons of each suggestion.

9. **Move forward.** Agree to try a resolution without resentment and give it your full effort.

10. **Forgive.** Holding onto anger and resentment is not helpful or useful. It hurts us and burdens relationships. Forgive yourself and others for being different and for having an argument or disagreement. Accept the idea that by learning to resolve conflict, we grow as people.

The following mindfulness exercises can help you to identify physical sensations that you interpret as specific emotions. Start now, right where you are, by checking in with yourself.

## Start Where You Are

Wherever you are, stop and focus on the physical sensations in your body.
If you like, close your eyes.
Or keep your eyes open and turn your awareness inward.

Notice your breathing. Is it fast? Slow? Deep? Shallow?
Notice your beating heart.
Feel the sensations in your stomach.
Are your muscles tense anywhere?
Does anything feel uncomfortable?
Does anything feel pleasant?
Can you simply sit with these sensations and stay aware of them,
    breathing calmly?
Can you notice how these sensations change?

"A lot of times I'm angry, and that's just a cover emotion for when I'm sad. You're angry for so long, and then you realize you're just sad. Then you have to think about what you're sad about. And then I sit in it, for a really long time. A lot of the time, sadness is just overwhelming and all you can do is be sad."

—Grace P., high school student

Now ask yourself if you are experiencing an emotion. Accept anything
   that comes.

| | |
|---|---|
| Are you angry? | Anxious? |
| Peaceful? | Depressed? |
| Happy? | Disgusted? |
| Sad? | Proud? |
| Excited? | Annoyed? |
| Afraid? | Resentful? |
| Ashamed? | Something else? |

How do you know what emotion you're feeling?
From a physical sensation?
From a thought?

Make a mental note of the emotion you are feeling, and ask yourself how
   you know you're feeling it.
Accept whatever emotion you notice—no need for judgment. This emotion
   is simply what you are experiencing at this time.

   If you did this exercise and could not figure out what you were
feeling, you are probably not alone. Sometimes we go around with a
vague sense of unease. We might act grouchy, sad, or irritable without
realizing it. One clue that this is happening is that people keep asking
you what's wrong—and you don't really know. Then tap into yourself
with these exercises. Slowing down and paying attention to your
emotions can help you identify and work with them. The more you
practice these exercises, the more you may be able to tolerate difficult

emotions without reacting negatively to them. Here's another exercise to try:

## Observing Your Emotion

Sit in a meditation posture, and start by taking three mindful breaths.
Notice the expansion and contraction of your chest and belly as
    you breathe.
Relax more and more with each breath.
Imagine sinking deeply into your seat.

Take a moment to imagine yourself as an empty balloon.
You are hollow.
Notice what that emptiness feels like.
Breathe into it.

Notice the emotions you are experiencing.
What events or thoughts triggered the emotions?
Can you find the point when these emotions began?
What physical sensations did you have when you started feeling this way?
Are you having the same thoughts and sensations now?
Are they more or less intense than when they started?

Imagine your emotion as a small pet that needs your attention.
Can you sit with this pet on your lap?
Imagine holding it still, with kindness.
Be caring and patient with your emotion pet.

Allow your emotion to rest where it is, accepted and unjudged.
If your emotion feels too strong, end this exercise here.
If your emotion calms down, keep breathing into the hollow space
    inside you.
Either way, end your meditation when you are ready.

Being patient and gentle with yourself and your emotions is one way to let them settle on their own. Your emotions do not have to define you. Just as you are not your thoughts, you are also not your emotions.

You may go through times when you feel such an intense emotion—anger or sadness, for example—that you can barely sit still. If that happens, try this exercise for holding the "heat" of your emotion.

## Holding the Heat of an Emotion

Sit in a meditation posture, or stand if you prefer.

Take three mindful breaths. Notice the expansion and contraction of your chest and belly as you breathe.

Relax more and more with each breath.

Focus on the strong emotion you feel.

Rub your hands together to feel the friction of this emotion in your hands.

Breathing in, make two fists, squeezing them tight to gather this emotion into your hands.

Breathing out, open your palms and release the energy of the emotion.

Hold your hands in front of you, as if you are holding a ball of emotion.

Breathe in and move your hands apart, allowing the emotion ball to expand.

Breath out and move your hands closer together, allowing the emotion ball to contract.

Watch your hands moving out and in as you breathe. Repeat several times.

As you move your hands, notice that you are keeping your emotions safe between your hands.

Does the energy of your emotion change as you do this exercise?

Continue as long as you are comfortable.

When you are done, shake out your hands to release any tension and any lingering emotions.

Or wash your hands in cool water and imagine the emotion rinsing away.

"If I'm mad, I try not to act out in the worst way possible because I don't want to hurt other people's feelings. I care about other people. If someone feels hurt, I'll try to comfort them. If I'm angry, I try to talk to you about why I'm angry. I'll explain to them in depth why I'm mad. That usually calms me down because if I get everything off my chest, then there's nothing there."

—Balseba T., high school student

Sometimes emotions motivate us. Other times they drag us down. But emotions themselves are not the problem. What we *do* with our emotions is key. For example, your negative emotions in the school hallway could motivate you to lash out. Or they could motivate you to do something positive instead, such as starting an anti-bullying campaign or a mindfulness group at school.

A reminder: If meditation isn't helping and you feel you cannot handle your emotions alone, find a person you trust—a friend, teacher, parent, or counselor—and share your feelings. Talking out emotions can be an important step toward happiness.

# THE TAKEAWAY

Emotions are part of our human experience, and we make them from our perceptions and attitudes. Something happens, and our body and chemicals in our brain respond to the trigger. We feel physical sensations. These sensations color our perception of a situation. We

"If you've ever been to the ocean . . . if you've ever been caught under a wave, and you feel the water going over you, that's what anxiety is. You're just stuck there, watching and feeling waves go over you."

—Grace P., high school student

interpret the sensations as an emotion—anger, fear, disgust, sadness, or enjoyment, for example. As we experience emotion, we react to it. Sometimes our reactions are quick. Other times, they are delayed. If we slow down and explore our emotions and add awareness, we can become skilled at responding wisely to whatever emotions we experience.

Your emotions don't have to control you. You can control them.

# 5
# STRESSED OUT:
# A BODY-MIND CONNECTION

Did you grab this book because you're stressed out? Maybe you feel stress when you think about all the homework you have to do or about pressure to get good grades. You may be so stressed about schoolwork that you put it off or don't do it at all. And you know where that gets you!

For some people, school pressure can create panic attacks. One young woman experienced daily panic attacks that sometimes seemed to come out of nowhere. She would feel her heart beating very fast, and she would start to hyperventilate. She felt as if she was in danger, and she could focus only on the fear in her mind and her difficulty breathing. Everything else around her was a blur. Other people may experience a panic attack with light-headedness, nausea, physical agitation, chest tightness, hot or cold flashes, sweating, and racing thoughts. They might fear they will lose control or faint.

People commonly feel stress and anxiety when they cannot control their situations. If your family is in financial difficulty or your parents are going through a divorce, for example, you might feel stress every day. If you're bullied or assaulted or picked on because of your race, religion, gender, or any other trait, you might have constant stress. Or maybe you or someone you care about has health problems that feel overwhelming. You aren't sure how to cope. All of these very real issues can weigh you down and leave little room for calm or for happiness.

## WHAT CAUSES YOU STRESS?

"School! Everything about school. It's just a stressful situation. The bell rings, and it's like, 'Oh no!' It feels like everything you're doing is, kind of, being watched . . . by teachers. If you mess up, they will see. They will know. And there will be some sort of unknown repercussion."

—Grace P., high school student

"Get good grades! Get good grades! I have a very creative mind that's art oriented, and I can't get good grades in just about anything. . . . I had a panic attack at school, which was *so* not fun at all. In my head, it kind of sounds like there's someone there telling me I'm not good enough. I just kept panicking."

—Artemis, high school student

"When people yell, I don't like that. That makes me stressed. If someone starts yelling, I'm like, 'Can you please calm down?' Because that's too much. My brain can't handle it. Physically, I get really bad headaches. And emotionally, it feels like my heart's just dropping because I don't like it when people yell. If you're yelling at someone, it feels like you're putting so much anger toward them."

—Balseba T., high school student

# STRESS IN YOUR BODY

When we talk about stress, we usually think of it as a negative. Neurologists and psychologists point out that the mind and body experience two types of stress: positive stress—called eustress—and negative stress, or distress. We experience both types through physical sensations.

Eustress is the body's short-term psychological response to a positive, healthy stress such as getting excited and motivated for a game or performance. We can also experience eustress when we're having fun riding a roller coaster, trying a new sport, or solving a puzzle. Eustress releases feel-good chemicals called endorphins in the brain. They give us energy and help us focus and perform better. And through eustress, we have a sense of fun or satisfaction. Just the right amount of stress is actually good for the brain too. Eustress can enhance the growth of neurons (nerve cells) in the hippocampus, a structure in the brain that forms memories.

Stress isn't all bad. The excitement you might feel before competing in an athletic contest, for instance, is called eustress. It helps motivate you to do well. Distress, on the other hand, can lead to emotional and even physical pain.

But distress is not fun. When we are frightened, overwhelmed, or sad, we may experience distress as unpleasant physical sensations. Distress can trigger headaches, stomachaches, and muscle cramps. It can also cause restlessness and insomnia. Some people get so upset or nervous that they can't eat or they throw up. What's causing these symptoms?

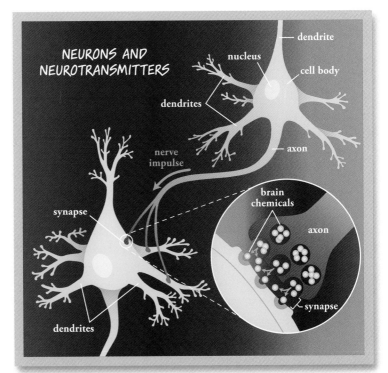

This infographic shows neurons in the brain, their major structures, and how they connect to one another. The spaces between neurons are called synapses. By crossing synapses, brain chemicals such as dopamine and serotonin travel from one neuron to the next.

# THE STRESS RESPONSE

Neurobiological studies show that when people are exposed to a threat, their brain and body react with the fight-or-flight response. They physically prepare to either fight off the danger or to run from it. Imagine hiking up a mountain trail, and suddenly, you see a rattlesnake in front of you on the path, poised to strike. Your heart starts pounding, and your muscles tense up. Your stomach does flip-flops. Your body is getting ready to fight or flee.

The stress response begins in the brain. When you are in a stressful situation (such as an encounter with a rattlesnake), the body's sense organs—the eyes and ears, in particular—pick up and send information to the amygdala, a structure in the brain that processes emotion. The amygdala then interprets the information and, sensing threat, sends signals to the hypothalamus, which helps control the

## HOW DO YOU HANDLE YOUR STRESS?

"I usually do some breathing exercises because I get a lot of homework, which causes a lot of stress, so I want to calm down. Me and my mom sometimes practice yoga together. Deep breathing and meditation really help me calm down and focus on a personal level."

—Adam Avin, high school student

"I have social anxiety, so in crowds it feels like an out of body experience, like you're floating above it when you can't get out. I try to close my eyes and block out sound. I try to pretend I'm not there. Singing songs helps too. If you focus on what you're singing, it gets your mind off of where you are. I'm singing in my head, and it kind of blocks out the surroundings. And it, I guess, brings me back. It doesn't fix everything, but it helps me not think about it."

—Mae H., high school student

body's nervous system. The hypothalamus triggers the adrenal glands. These small structures on top of the kidneys release epinephrine (also known as adrenaline) into the bloodstream. This hormone is one of many chemicals that help our bodies function. In a fight-or-flight situation, epinephrine causes the heart to beat faster, pushing blood to the muscles and vital organs. Pulse and blood pressure go up, and breathing gets faster. Extra oxygen goes to the brain, which increases alertness. The pupils dilate (widen), which allows more light into the eyes for better vision. Also, the muscles tense up, making the body ready for action. The adrenal glands also secrete the hormone cortisol. It stimulates the breakdown of glycogen (a substance stored in the liver and muscles) into glucose, a sugar that fuels the body. This process gives the body energy. The person is ready to fight the danger or flee for safety.

The fight-or-flight response is an essential survival mechanism for humans. It was helpful in prehistoric times, when humans lived in small clans in the wild, fighting off animals and running for shelter from storms. This response is still helpful when we face danger. Maybe a fire starts in the kitchen, and you must react quickly to put out the flames. Or perhaps you're riding a bike and have to swerve quickly to avoid a dog running into your path. This response in the brain happens so quickly that you may not be aware of it. People often react and escape danger before they realize what's happening.

# STRESS WITHOUT THE RATTLESNAKE

The downside of this autonomic response to danger is that sometimes the body perceives a threat when there is no rattlesnake—a false alarm. Common situations such as taking an exam, speaking in public, or joining a new social group can cause this stress response. Some people feel distress in many other types of situations. They may feel stress throughout much of their day.

Chronic activation of the stress response can harm the body. When we're scared or nervous, we sometimes take fast and shallow breaths. This can cause dizziness. In people who have asthma, it can trigger an asthma attack. Acute emotional stress can also increase the heart rate and, over time, damage the heart. Continuous overactivation of the nervous system can also cause high blood glucose levels, which is unhealthy for people with diabetes. It can also cause insomnia. Chronic stress can also cause changes in the brain that impair learning, memory, and mood.

"In old castles, they had like a chained gate that they let down and nothing could get through. When I'm stressed, it feels like a gate's going down and I can't do anything. It's like I'm on the outside, and the concept is on the inside. So it's like I'm trying to get to the concept but the stress is just stopping me."

—E. Parnell, high school student

Mindfulness can help. Research shows that mindfulness is associated with lower levels of cortisol and other stress hormones. Research also suggests that mindfulness helps people relax and manage chronic stress. Most scientists agree that more research is needed to fully understand how mindfulness interventions change the brain and body.

The following exercises are helpful in managing the physical symptoms experienced during distress. Try this one when you feel distress, no matter where you are:

## Full Belly Breaths

Pause and focus on your breathing.
Take full, deep breaths through your nose and into your belly.
Breathe out forcefully through your mouth, and let all the air go.
You could also make a whoosh sound out loud if you wish.

Continue taking deep inbreaths, giving your body the oxygen it needs.
When you are ready to exhale, strongly expel all the air out, letting your
    lungs have room for fresh air.

When you're ready, slow down your breathing.
Breathe in and out through your nose.
Count to five as you breathe: *in*-two-three-four-five.
Hold your breath and count: *hold*-two-three-four-five.
Count to eight as you exhale: *out*-two-three-four-five-six-seven-eight.

Do this breathing sequence (in, hold, out) six times.
Keep your breath slow and gentle, and focus your mind on your counting.
End this exercise after the sixth sequence or when you feel ready.

Deep abdominal breathing engages the vagus nerve—a nerve that runs from the brain stem (a structure at the base of the brain) to the abdomen. Among other functions, the vagus nerve stimulates a relaxation response in your body. The next exercise adds body awareness to full belly breaths, which can pull your attention away from upsetting thoughts and focus it on your body and the place where you are.

## Awareness

Sit in a meditation posture, and start by taking three mindful breaths.
Notice the expansion and contraction of your chest and belly as
    you breathe.
Relax more and more with each breath.
Imagine sinking deeply into your seat.

As you breathe mindfully, notice how your body makes contact with the
    space around it.
Tap your right foot on the floor three times. *Tap, tap, tap.*
Then tap your left foot on the floor three times. *Tap, tap, tap.*
Tap your right hand on a surface next to you three times. *Tap, tap, tap.*
Then tap your left hand on a surface next to you three times. *Tap,
    tap, tap.*
Tap both feet on the floor and your hands on the surface next to you
    three times.
*Tap, tap, tap.*

Next, holding your palms together in front of you, tap the tips of your
    thumbs together three times. *Tap, tap, tap.*
Then tap the tips of your index fingers together three times. *Tap,
    tap, tap.*
Then tap your middle fingers, ring fingers, and pinkies together one after
    the other.
*Tap, tap, tap.*
Tap to feel connected to your body and the space around you.

Do this exercise as many times as you like, always breathing mindfully.
It can help bring your attention to the present moment.
End this exercise when you wish.

For deeper relaxation, try this full body-scan exercise. You'll want to find a quiet place to lie down.

## Body Scan

Lie down on a mat on the floor or on a couch or bed.

If possible, remove your shoes and socks.

Put a pillow, rolled towel, or yoga block under the back of your head. You can also rest your head on a book with a sweater or towel on top for cushioning.

Stretch out your legs. Touch your ankles together, and let your feet fall away from each other.

Adjust your position until you are comfortable, with your arms by your side.

You could close your eyes or keep them open, whichever way helps you relax.

The purpose of this exercise is to bring awareness to any tension in your body.

Start by taking three soft, slow mindful breaths.

Then bring awareness to your toes and feet.

You may want to wiggle your toes or flex your feet for a second and then stop.

Notice all the sensations in your feet.

Take your time and gradually move your attention up to your calves.

Then slowly focus on your knees, thighs, and hips.

You can squeeze the muscles in each area and then release them.

Squeezing and releasing helps you notice any area where you could be holding tension.

Pay attention to the sensations in your legs after you release your muscles.

Slowly bring your attention to your torso.

What sensations do you notice? Is anything tight?

Squeeze and release the muscles in your back and abdomen.

Then focus on the feeling of sinking into the surface beneath you.

Relax into it.

Gradually move your attention to your shoulders, arms, and hands.

Again, squeeze your muscles tight for a second and then release.

Do you notice any tightness in your arms or hands?

Are your fingers relaxed?


Then pay attention to your neck, jaw, face, and head.

Clench your jaw and squeeze your facial muscles tight for a second.
    Then release.

Open your mouth as wide as you can, stretching your facial muscles, and
    then close your mouth.

What do you notice when you relax your facial muscles?


Rest and allow your awareness to go to your whole body.

Are you relaxed from your toes to your head?

If you feel any tightness, breathe deeply and direct your attention to
    this spot?

Squeeze and release those muscles three times.

Let your body and mind rest and recover.


When you are ready to end this exercise, wiggle your fingers and toes.

If your eyes were closed, open them.

Stretch out your arms and legs. Yawn if you wish.

Gradually expand your awareness to the room around you.


If you choose to get up, slowly roll to your side and then stand.

Try to move without rushing.

Take your awareness of your breath and body with you as you go about
    the rest of your day or evening.

When we are anxious, we might feel physically unbalanced—a little wobbly. A great way to counteract this feeling is with balancing exercises. The following one is a timed exercise, so use a kitchen timer or a smartphone timer:

## Be the Mountain

Stand with your feet slightly apart. Place equal weight on the balls and heels of your feet.

Raise your arms over your head, shoulder width apart and fingers spread wide.

Stay in this posture for two minutes, if you can.

Practice deep belly breathing as you stand.

You can choose to make a sound with each exhalation, if you wish.

Keep your attention on the bottom of your feet.

Feel the floor or the ground beneath you, holding you safe.

After two minutes, drop your arms and swing them loosely forward and back three times.

Another way to calm your nervous system and find inner balance is with a yoga position called the child's pose.

## Child's Pose

Choose a quiet spot on a carpeted floor or yoga mat.

Start on your hands and knees, with your legs hip-distance apart.

Then shift your position so your big toes are touching. Your hips and knees will spread apart naturally.

Your hands should be directly under your shoulders.

Exhale and draw your buttocks downward toward the floor.

Allow your torso to rest on or between your thighs, with your forehead on the carpet or yoga mat.

Extend your arms alongside your head and forward, keeping them long and relaxed. Press a little into the carpet or mat with your hands and fingers.

If you aren't able to get your buttocks all the way to your heels, place a rolled-up towel in between your buttocks and heels for support.

While in this position, close your eyes if you wish and breathe into your belly through your nose.

As you exhale, let your weight sink into your hands. Focus on your back gently rising and falling with each in-and-out cycle of breathing.

Relax your jaws, and feel the breath at the back of your throat as you inhale and exhale.

Stay in the pose as long as it feels comfortable.

When you want to come out of the pose, slowly walk your hands up to your thighs and sit up. Open your eyes if they were closed.

Sit back on your heels before you stand, and take a couple of gentle breaths to conclude the exercise.

# PAIN

Physical pain is an interaction of sensory nerves, the spinal cord, and the brain. Without the ability to feel physical pain, you wouldn't pull your hand away from a hot stove or know when you had injured yourself. So you could say that physical pain is a valuable response to tissue damage to your body.

But physical pain is unpleasant, and sometimes it's so great that you can't think of anything else. You might obsess about the pain, worrying that it's not going away or that it's signaling a more serious health problem. Worrying about pain adds emotional suffering to physical suffering. And emotional suffering can make the physical situation worse. Physical pain and emotional suffering activate the same areas of the brain—the anterior insula and the anterior cingulate cortex. So sometimes it's hard to figure out how much something hurts physically, hurts emotionally, or both.

Whenever you feel physical pain—such as a headache—try this exercise to determine the difference between your physical sensations of pain and your emotional suffering. Remember, though, that this exercise is for becoming more aware of your body and emotions. It is not a substitute for medical care. If your physical pain is acute or it continues, seek medical attention.

## Physical Pain or Emotional Suffering?

Lie down on a mat on the floor or on a couch or bed.

If possible, remove your shoes and socks.

Put a pillow, rolled towel, or yoga block under the back of your head. You can also rest your head on a book with a sweater or towel for cushioning.

Adjust your position until you are comfortable, with your arms by your side.

Stretch out your legs. Touch your heels together, and let your feet fall away from each other.

Close your eyes or keep them open, whichever way helps you relax.

Focus your attention on your body.

Try a body scan to find a part of your body that has no pain and is loose and relaxed.

What do the muscles of this area feel like?

How about the skin? Is that pain-free?

Rest your attention on this pain-free area for a few moments.

Move your attention to the area where you feel pain.

What are the physical sensations you are experiencing?

Do you feel throbbing, stinging, stabbing, or aching?

Is the pain on your skin or deep inside your body?

Does the pain come in waves?

What makes it worse or better?

Notice your attitude toward your pain.
Do you feel frustrated and want to push it away?
Do you feel embarrassed about having pain?
Do you feel worried or victimized by pain?
Or do you feel calm about your pain?

Explore your thoughts and emotions about this pain.
Do your thoughts make you feel better or worse?
Does your physical pain trigger strong emotions such as worry or anger?
Explore with care and gentleness.

Return your attention to your whole body.
Can you find another place where you feel no pain?
What happens when you focus your attention there?
Do your thoughts and emotions change?
Can you relax a little by focusing on a pain-free area?

Use the strength of your mind and breath to help ease your pain.
Breathe gently and evenly, and allow your breath to help you relax.
Use your imagination to see yourself in a beautiful, calming place—perhaps
    on a beach, in a quiet forest, or in a tub of warm water.
Or imagine a soothing rainstorm or the waves of water lapping against
    a shore.
Or imagine you are drifting on a puffy cloud through the sky.

Rest this way for as long as you like if it feels soothing.
End this exercise when you are ready by opening your eyes and taking a
    few gentle breaths in and out.
When you want to get up, roll over to your side and stand up slowly.

This exercise might help interrupt the stress response and lessen your
emotional pain. By working through or letting go of your emotional
suffering, you might even be able to reduce your physical pain.

# 6
# ANYBODY LISTENING?
# MINDFULNESS AND SOCIAL MEDIA

You've got it in your pocket or purse. It's never far away, calling for your constant attention: "Look at me! Look at me!" Yup, we're talking about your smartphone—that little box that can stir up social media drama any time of the day or night. Is it your friend or foe?

According to polls, some teens (45 percent) say social media has neither a positive nor a negative effect on their lives. Others (31 percent) think social media is all positive. They like having quick access to news, and they feel empowered by being part of online communities. They can connect to friends easily. A smaller group (24 percent) of teens thinks social media has a mostly negative impact on their lives.

Having a phone is a big distraction for some people, especially when they have to do homework or concentrate on an important task

Studies show that texting and participating in social media can lead to anxiety and self-criticism. Use your mindfulness practice to review and modify your relationship to your devices. You may find that by cutting back on social media and texting, you feel less stressed out.

or at the workplace. Others feel bad about themselves when they use social media because they compare themselves physically to others in online photos and worry they don't look as good. Knowing that people filter and manipulate photos doesn't lessen their negative feelings. Or they see their peers together in online photos and feel excluded. Some say that with social media, bullies have a bigger platform and can spread rumors faster than they could before smartphones were invented.

Because social media is so portable, immediate, and constant, it amplifies the negative effects of rumor and judgment. And devices can cause social disconnect. Most of us know what it feels like when we're trying to talk to someone, but we find them staring at their smartphone instead, totally absorbed in digital life.

## WHAT THE EXPERTS SAY

Researchers say that electronic devices have positive and negative effects on well-being. According to Jean Twenge, professor of psychology at

## WHAT ARE THE UPSIDES TO SOCIAL MEDIA?

"What I like about it [social media] the most is that whenever you're lonely or something, you can access your friends really quickly."

—Beatrice E., high school student

"I go on YouTube for a lot of comedy, because I like to laugh. A lot. I usually look up riddles. There's a whole channel that has them."

—Balseba T., high school student

"I try to follow really uplifting pages, like happy quotes and really motivational things. And so, when I've had a really bad day, it's nice to get on social media and watch really stupid videos of dogs, and that lifts my mood."

—E. Parnell, high school student

"I think social media can make me feel a bit sluggish, a bit slow. Maybe it makes me feel more relaxed, so I don't feel like doing much else when I'm on my phone."

Dominic C., high school student

San Diego State University, "The arrival of the smartphone has radically changed every aspect of teenagers' lives, from the nature of their social interactions to their mental health." She says that some of the changes are positive, some are negative, and many are both. Twenge's research shows that twenty-first-century teenagers go out with friends less often than previous generations, learn to drive later, have sex for the first time later, and are less likely to work in after-school jobs. One reason for these delays is that teens are staying home and hanging out on devices instead of going out and trying new activities. That homebody behavior might keep teens physically safer and reduce the likelihood of teen pregnancies, but Twenge believes that teens are more at risk for psychological distress than were those of previous generations. "There is compelling evidence that the devices we've placed in young people's hands are having profound effects on their lives—and making them seriously unhappy," says Twenge.

## HOW MUCH IS TOO MUCH?

Other researchers say that moderate screen use probably doesn't harm teens and they may benefit emotionally from the social connections online. That's good news for people who check in daily but don't stay glued to their phone. But young adults who spend two or more hours a day on social media are more likely to report feeling anxious and depressed than those who spend less time online. According to a report by the Royal Society for Public Health in the United Kingdom, Instagram and Snapchat have the strongest negative effects on the mental health of young people. One reason is that teens compare their looks to images of others (sometimes digitally enhanced or filtered) on these platforms and often feel bad if they think they don't measure up. They also compare the number of engagements of their own posts to those of others, and they often feel bad if few people like or comment on their posts.

Psychologists and psychiatrists say that some teens are actually addicted to their phones. Signs of addiction include the inability to resist using the phone and anxiety when the phone is not available for use. Teens who are addicted to their phones have significantly higher levels of depression, anxiety, insomnia, and impulsivity (acting with little or no forethought or reflection) than nonaddicted teens. Researchers have also found an imbalance of brain chemistry in teens addicted to smartphones. Addicted teenagers have higher than normal amounts of a brain chemical called gamma-aminobutyric acid. Side effects of these increased levels include drowsiness and anxiety.

# USING DIGITAL DEVICES MINDFULLY

Perhaps you experience only positive effects from using social media, and you ask, "What's the big deal?" But if you've ever scrolled through social media and come away feeling sluggish, unhappy, or unable to sleep, you might want to explore your personal connection to your electronic devices and to social media. Start by taking the following self-assessment and trying the mindfulness exercise afterward:

## Social Media Self-Assessment

This assessment is meant to help you to think about your connection to your phone and social media—both the positives and the negatives. Write down your answers. When you are done, make a tally of the number of positive and negative responses.

- Do you check your phone as soon as you wake up?
- Do you feel a constant urge to check your phone?
- Do you go on social media for more than two hours per day?
- Does going online ever change your mood?
- Do you use social media to forget about personal problems?
- If going online changes your mood, does it usually change it for the better?
- Do you use your device at mealtime?
- Can you become so focused on your device that you ignore what's happening around you?
- Are you ever so engaged by social media that you neglect homework or other obligations?
- Do you ever say no to doing things with friends or family because you want to hang out on your phone or other device?
- Do you feel more connected to other people when you check social media?
- Do you organize social events on social media?
- Do you use your phone or social media for creative or artistic projects?

- Do you use social media to stay informed about a special area of interest, such as sports, music, theater, art, politics, or science?
- Would you be annoyed if you couldn't look up information online whenever you wanted to?
- Do you feel anxious when your smartphone is out of battery power?
- Do you feel anxious if you don't have your smartphone with you?
- Do you walk and text or post at the same time?
- If you drive, do you ever text or look at social media while driving?
- Do you say whatever you want on social media?
- Do you worry about backlash if you post something honest or controversial?
- Do you stress about your online image?
- Do you compare your social media feed to the feeds of other people?
- Do you focus on the number of likes or engagements with your post?
- Do you ever feel bad about yourself or about your life after looking at social media?
- Do you ever have trouble going to bed because you don't want to get off social media?
- Do you ever have trouble falling asleep because you're thinking about something on social media?

If you find that negative responses outweigh positives for you, the following mindfulness exercises can help. (If the assessment makes you worry that you might even have an addiction to your phone, you could take this assessment to a counselor or doctor to discuss it.)

No matter how much we love our smart devices, they can get in the way of being in the present. Sometimes the present is boring or tedious, so grabbing your phone may feel like a great escape.

# ARE THERE DOWNSIDES TO USING SOCIAL MEDIA?

"The phone can be a stressor. I recognize it is not really that healthy to be worrying about Instagram and Snapchat and things like that. But sometimes I think, 'Oh, other people's pictures are better than the one I just posted, or they have more likes or got more comments than I did.' And sometimes if you have free time, you'll unconsciously just take out your phone and check Instagram. I will admit that I wake up and quickly check Instagram and Snapchat. Like, that's kind of the first thing I do. I spend a lot of time on Instagram, probably more than I should. It's become a habit."

—Maggie S., high school student

"I'm distracted. I don't realize all the cool things that are happening around me. I'll be so in depth on a book on my phone that I don't realize we just passed up, like, the coolest tree. Or, I'll be scrolling through Instagram and I don't realize that my grandparents just walked in the door. I'll realize it after five minutes, and I'll be, like, 'Oh my goodness, I'm a horrible person. I didn't realize my grandparents just walked in.' So, I'll throw my phone to my bed and go downstairs and hang out with them."

—Elizabeth Grace, high school student

"It gets so dramatic very easily on social media. I find that when something happens over social media, people tend to think that you're trying to avoid them in some sort of way. And it adds extra layers that aren't necessary. When you go into school and see them in person, you're not really sure what to do because you're not really sure what just happened on the phone. They could pretend it never happened or they could keep pretending it's happening. You don't really know how to gauge it."

—Beatrice E., high school student

"If I'm hanging out with my friends, and they're always on social media, it gets kind of aggravating because they're like 'Yeah, yeah, yeah, we can do that later.' I would rather be going to do something outside compared to sitting inside all day when it's nice outside."

—Alexander B., high school student

Other times, you might mindlessly check your phone out of habit. You might get sucked into social media and miss connecting more meaningfully to other people and to yourself. The next exercise will help you think about why you're checking your phone. Do this exercise before checking it:

## Before Checking Your Phone

Holding your phone, take three mindful breaths. Notice the expansion and contraction of your chest and belly as you breathe. Relax more and more with each breath.

Stop and ask yourself, "Why do I really want to check my phone right now?" If you wait a second or two, you may find the urge to check the phone passes.

Then ask yourself, "Am I obsessing about something?" Explore the obsession to see if it's something that requires attention or if it's a sudden impulse that you can redirect through mindful breathing.

Do a body scan and ask, "What am I feeling in my body?" If you are feeling a strong emotion, you might have physical sensations tied to it. Is your body relaxed and calm? Or do you feel heavy and sluggish? Are your muscles tight? What other physical sensations do you have? Are they connected to your emotions?

Look around and find one interesting thing to focus on. It could be something in your favorite color, a favorite picture, or a pet you love. Focus on that thing for thirty seconds to build a sense of calm and happiness. This helps you focus on the present and to notice where you are, so you don't lose yourself in the virtual world.

Try asking yourself, "What do others around me need right now?" You may find that it's more important to help out than to look at your phone.

When you communicate by texting, you miss out on subtle social cues, such as facial expressions and the speaker's tone of voice. Using images, such as emojis and GIFs, can help. But they don't take the place of in-person communication. Take breaks from your phone to improve relationships with friends and family.

By doing this exercise, you may decide that you do want or need to look at your phone. If you do decide to use your phone, check back in with yourself afterward. Ask yourself, "How do I feel now?" Do you have a sense of satisfaction about accomplishing something important on your phone? Are you happy about having talked to a friend? Did you read something meaningful on social media? Or do you feel anxious or unhappy? Return to the exercise occasionally or even regularly to check in with yourself about your relationship with your device. Here's another exercise to help you explore your connection with your phone:

## Conscious Connection

Sit in a mindful position, and hold your phone in your hands.
Put your phone on Do Not Disturb, and click off the home screen.
Start by taking three mindful breaths.

Notice the expansion and contraction of your chest and belly as
   you breathe.
Relax more and more with each breath.
Imagine sinking deeply into your seat.

Feel the weight of your phone in your hands.
Notice if you have an urge to look down and turn your phone back on.
If you don't have an urge, rest in that calm space.
Close your eyes, and notice the sounds around you.

If or when you have an urge to use your phone, ask yourself, "What is
   driving the urge?"
Is it a physical sensation?
Is it a thought?
Is it an emotion?
Watch that sensation, thought, or emotion to see if it shifts.
Become curious about it.
Ask yourself, "Isn't it interesting that I am drawn to my phone?"
Ask yourself, "How did this urge begin?"

Squeeze your phone, and notice the sensation.
Ask yourself, "Does this small device help me feel happier?"
If it doesn't, reflect on why you want to use it.
Does it change the way you see yourself?
Do you want to change something about the way you use your phone?
Do you want to control your phone or let it control you?

Focus on your breathing again.
Open your eyes, and take in the place where you are sitting.
Consciously make a choice whether to use your phone right away or not.
Bring your focused attention with you into whatever you decide to do
   after you end this exercise.

## MINDFULNESS ON YOUR PHONE

There are many ways to add a smartphone to your mindfulness practice. You can use a mindfulness or meditation app that guides you through breathing exercises or visualizations. You'll find a list of such apps in the Further Information section at the end of this book. You can also go online and watch YouTube videos that guide you through mindfulness exercises.

Meditating with your cell phone is a way of bringing awareness to how you use your device. It slows you down so you can make a conscious choice about when to use your phone or device.

Another way to approach your device mindfully is to take breaks from it. For example, instead of checking your phone for a break as you do homework, stand and stretch or do a short mindful walk around your room. Do a few squats or jumping jacks, go outside, or poke your head out a window for a few moments of fresh air. Here are some other ideas to try:

- Take a timed break from your phone on a weekend day. Start with half an hour or an hour at any point in the day or evening hours. Work up over a period of weeks to more timed breaks from your device.
- Turn off all sounds and notifications on your phone for an hour on any day you choose. Once that becomes easier, try doing it for several hours, then eventually a whole day.
- Choose a day to send only a limited number of text messages. You choose the number. See if you can do this more regularly every week. As it becomes more familiar, you may find yourself texting less.
- Choose a day to have only face-to-face conversations. Don't text at all.

Set aside time each day or each week for connecting in person—without using devices to communicate.

If you try any of these ideas, remember to tell your friends and family about your break, so they won't be concerned when you don't answer your phone. And let them know how they can contact you in an emergency.

## FACE-TO-FACE OR BEHIND THE SCREEN?

Sometimes you'd rather talk on social media than face-to-face. Messaging is fast and easy, and you can communicate privately, without anyone overhearing. Maybe you have something difficult to say, and you'd rather not look someone else in the eye when you communicate this information. Or maybe it's simpler to send out a group message than calling or texting individuals about the same thing.

But then sometimes you're joking in a message and the other person doesn't get the joke. When you don't see facial expressions or hear a tone of voice, you can easily mistake a joke for an insult. Sometimes when you say something, an online conflict flares up. Or you read a message from a friend and don't respond, and they think you're ignoring them, resulting in hurt or angry feelings. Most of us are on the go and want to get our messages out fast. But oops! We put in an awkward typo or didn't mean what we texted or we sent it to the wrong person.

Slow chatting—or chatting with mindfulness—is one way to make sure we say what we mean and mean what we say on social media. Try this exercise for an introduction to slow chat:

## Mindful Slow Chat

When you receive a text, read it first. Then pause before you type a reply.

Take three mindful breaths.
Notice the expansion and contraction of your chest and belly as you breathe.
Relax more and more with each breath.
Imagine sinking deeply into your seat.

Check your thoughts and emotions.
Before you text back, ask yourself, What is my purpose in responding to this message?
Imagine the other person or people receiving your message.
How do you want them to react? Are you making accurate assumptions about how they will react?
What is your intention?
Pause.

Type your message.
Pause.
Reread it.
Pause.

Remind yourself of the purpose for sending the message. Make any changes you think will improve your messaging.

Decide whether to send or delete it. You may realize that sending your text will cause more harm than good. Then it's smart to delete it.

The more you practice these exercises, the more conscious you will be when you hold or use your device. You are in control!

# 7
# LET'S GET PHYSICAL: RISING, EATING, MOVING, AND SLEEPING

Some people think they don't have time to practice mindfulness. They don't have time to set aside for a formal seated breath meditation. But even without a formal meditation session, you can be mindful throughout your day. Mindfulness is about having awareness, wherever you are. You can bring mindfulness into your day in many ways. Start by paying attention to your patterns and habits and to the ways you relate to other people.

In the morning, are you eager to get going or do you dread the day the minute you open your eyes? Do you smile when you see people? Grunt? Launch into a story? Do you ask other people how they are doing? Do you eat the same things every day or walk the same way to school or work? What do you notice when you are on the go?

# MINDFUL RISING

Some days are frantic. We wake up and go! And we keep doing things all day until we collapse at night. Does your pattern keep you running from one thing to the next? Or do you have spare time in your day? If you have a free moment, what do you do? Do you check your smartphone? How about checking in with yourself instead? Here's an exercise for starting your day with mindfulness.

## Start at the Beginning

Wake up and take three mindful breaths.

Notice the expansion and contraction of your chest and belly as you breathe.

Relax more and more with each breath.

Set a positive intention for the day. It could be as simple as "I will smile every time I walk through a door" or "I will reframe negative thoughts toward compassion."

Here are some other ideas for starting your day with mindfulness:

- Wake up and notice three interesting sounds around you. Focus on one of them for a minute or two. Move on to the second one and then the third.
- Wake up and practice breath meditation. Start with a few minutes, and extend the time if you can.
- Walk through a room, and notice what you smell. Is it a pleasant smell? How does it make you feel? If it's a bad smell, how does it make you feel? Can you find a good smell to hold in your mind?
- Start a daily calendar, and schedule at least one activity that makes you feel good.
- Think about or write down three things or people you are grateful for.

- Read a passage from an inspiring book. You can read it quietly to yourself or aloud—or first one way then the other.
- Write your own inspiring passage. It could be about your mindful intention for the day or about how you want to interact with people or how you want to resolve a problem in a respectful, thoughtful way.
- Prepare and eat a healthy breakfast. Sit down to eat it, and take your time. Slow, mindful eating helps you digest your food better, set the pace for a day that is not rushed, and enjoy your food more.
- Read a joke each morning and laugh. Laughter resets the brain toward happiness.
- Take some time for an exercise routine. It could be simple stretches for ten minutes, a walk around the block, or a bike ride to school or a favorite destination.
- Set daily limits for screen time and start today. Most experts say to avoid more than two hours a day.
- Remind yourself of your intention during the day.

# MINDFUL EATING

Eating consciously is a great way to expand your mindfulness practice. Eating can be a source of joy or despair, depending upon your circumstances and your relationship to food. Some people eat when they feel emotional—angry, sad, or even excited and happy. Others deny themselves food to control their weight or practice self-discipline. Some are happy to eat with friends or family. Others might be ashamed of how much or how little they eat, and they don't want to eat in public or with others. If you are regularly overeating or undereating or bingeing and purging and the pattern is harming your health,

Mindfulness doesn't have to be limited to meditation sessions. You can practice mindfulness all day, from morning until bedtime.

mood, and the way you feel about yourself, seek help from a doctor or counselor. Help is out there, and you are not alone.

No matter what your relationship with food, you can improve it using mindfulness. Mindful eating can help you get proper nutrition and help you understand the connection between food and your emotions. Mindful eating can also help you develop awareness and compassion for people who don't have enough to eat and for the people who help bring food to your table. In mindful eating, you can reflect on the ingredients in your food, where those ingredients are grown, and who grew them, harvested them, and helped bring them from farm or factory to table.

The following exercises will get you started with mindful eating. Start by asking yourself questions to raise your awareness of your relationship to food.

## Before You Eat

Am I hungry?

On a scale of one to ten, how hungry am I?

What does my hunger feel like?

Am I eating because I feel a strong emotion?

Am I eating because I am bored?

Am I eating because the clock tells me it's time to eat, but I'm not hungry?

Here are more questions about your relationship to food. Ask them while you are eating.

## While You Eat

What am I paying attention to as I eat? Is it my food or something else?

Am I eating nutritious food?

If not, why am I eating what I'm eating?

Am I trying to control my body through my food choices?

Am I alone and hiding my eating?

Does eating make me feel better? Why or why not?

Am I paying attention to the colors and flavors of the foods I eat?

Am I chewing my food carefully or gulping it down?

Am I sitting down to eat?

Do I feel joy and gratitude for my food?

This next exercise is a way to help you slow down as you eat and focus on what you are eating. Use a raisin or any other small piece of food.

## Simple Mindful Eating

Take a raisin and look at it in the palm of your hand.

Examine the creases in this small piece of food.

Hold it up to the light, and notice its colors.

Close your eyes, and use your sense of touch to explore the raisin.
Is it smooth or rough?
Hold the raisin close to your ear, and roll it around in your fingers.
Can you hear it making contact with your skin?

Smell the raisin.
What is the quality of its scent?
Notice if your mouth waters when you smell the raisin.
Does the smell make you think of something?
Do you like or dislike the taste of raisins?
Does your preference influence your thoughts right now?

Place the raisin on your tongue, but do not bite it.
Roll the raisin around in your mouth, and explore it with the tip of your tongue.
Notice the flavor it has before you bite it.
Is it sweet? Salty? Bitter?

Bite into the raisin slowly, and pay attention to the flavor.
Slowly chew this raisin, but do not swallow it right away.
Does the flavor change as you chew?

Finally, swallow the raisin and notice how it goes down your throat.
What taste does it leave behind?

Think about this exercise, asking yourself these questions:
How did eating the raisin slowly affect you?
Did you ever feel foolish during this exercise?
Was it boring to eat so slowly?
What other thoughts came up during this exercise?

# MICROMOVEMENTS

You can use mindfulness to notice all the ways you move, twist, bend, or hold yourself during the day. Notice if you bend your knees when you pick something up off the floor. Notice if you clench your jaw or grind your teeth when you sit in class. Notice if you walk with your head extending forward or if your spine is aligned. Such micromovements can contribute to muscle strain and injury, but they can also contribute to fitness and flexibility if you put them to work. Try these exercises:

- Sitting up straight in a chair, gently nod your head forward and back three times. With your left hand, gently pull the top right side of your head to the left until you feel a slight stretch. Do not pull hard. Hold the stretch for three seconds. Then use your right hand to gently stretch your head to the left and hold the stretch for three seconds. Repeat for another round if you wish.

- Sit in a chair, lean forward, bend at the waist, and gently stretch your lower back. Let your head, shoulders, and arms hang forward and loose. Hold there for ten to twenty seconds. Use your hands to push or pull yourself back up slowly.

- Press the palms of your hands together. Push your left palm against your right until you feel a stretch in your inner wrist. Then push your right palm against your left in the same manner. Move your palms forward and downward, keeping them together, with your elbows out, until you feel a stretch. Hold for five seconds and release.

- Lie down on a mat or towel. With your hands, gently grasp your legs just below your knees and pull them to your torso, with your ankles crossed and elbows pointing out to each side. You will feel a small stretch in your lower back. Breathe deeply and use your breath to relax your body. If your body is comfortable, you can gently roll your knees a little to the right and then slowly to the left. Do not force the stretch. When you are done, slowly release the grasp on your legs and stretch your legs out. Roll to your side, bend your knees, and slowly stand up.

- Sitting or standing, open your mouth and eyes as wide as you can. Stick out your tongue until you feel a stretch in your face muscles. Release. Repeat two more times.

"Taking a break is so important, because if you don't take a break, you're just going to be going and going and going. We're so wrapped up in these busy schedules that we don't realize that we need to take a break. I like to pull myself away and read comics and draw, and I play the ukulele. So it's really fun making music. And I love to dance. Whenever I dance, I kind of feel separated from that stress and anxiety. And I can express my emotions through dance."

*–Maggie S., high school student*

Notice how one small raisin can trigger many sensations. Notice, too, that the raisin's flavor changed as you chewed it. Did it start out sweet and then turn bitter?

If you want to expand on this mindful eating exercise, try it at any meal. Eat your first bite slowly and mindfully, noticing how the flavors and textures change as you chew. At the end of the meal, reflect on whether your first bite tasted different from the other bites. You may want to take more mindful bites with your next meal or practice the raisin exercise with a different food.

# MINDFUL MOVING

If you're an athlete, consider adding mindfulness to your workout routine. Studies show that athletes who practice mindfulness each day build mental resilience (the ability to respond positively to challenge and setback). This resilience helps them deal with hours of strenuous physical training. So sharpen your attention and open your awareness by practicing mindful breathing or meditation before your workout.

You can also focus on your breathing when you stretch before and after your workout or practice. Mindful stretching can increase your body awareness and flexibility, and it could also ease your recovery from any sports injuries.

Yoga is another form of movement that can expand your awareness and help focus your attention. Taking classes from a certified yoga instructor is the best way to learn. As you coordinate movement with breath, pay attention to the micromovements in your body, such as subtle twitches or muscle stretches and contractions. Treat yourself with compassion as you move. Your yoga practice is a mindfulness meditation in motion.

What if you don't play a sport or practice yoga? You can still add mindfulness to your daily movements. For instance, instead of jumping out of bed in the morning and hurrying into your day, wake up a minute or two earlier than usual. Pay attention to your movements as you roll over, lift your limbs, and plant your feet on the floor. Notice the tension in your leg muscles as you stand. Notice the small muscles in your feet as you move. This can be a perfect time of day to do some simple and slow stretches.

Brushing your teeth? Focus on the physical sensations of holding your toothbrush. Notice the bristles as they contact your teeth and gums. Feel the water as you swish it around your mouth and spit it out.

Taking a shower? This can be a great time to practice mindfulness. Notice your movements as you wash. Stay conscious of how the water streams down on your head. Imagine the water washing negative thoughts and emotions off you and sending them down the drain.

Taking a walk? Mindful walking is a traditional Buddhist practice. You pay attention to the movements in your body or concentrate on the small muscles in your feet as you walk. If you move with equipment such as braces or a wheelchair, you could focus on the way you make contact with the space around you or with the equipment itself. Notice your breathing as you move. Allow your gaze to be soft and expansive, noticing everything around you. If you start thinking about something, bring your focus back to your movements, to your muscles tightening and relaxing, and to your breath.

The aim of mindful movement is to focus your attention on the physical sensations of movement and expand your awareness of your environment. This can help you get out of your monkey mind and into the present.

Studies show that sleep is a must for physical and mental health. For a good night's sleep, keep all devices out of your bedroom. Calm yourself before bed by reading or doing a mind-clearing exercise.

## MINDFUL BEDTIME

What's your bedtime routine? Do you stay on your phone or electronic device until you crash? Do you take your device to bed with you? Do you stay up late doing homework and have trouble waking up for school? Do you have trouble falling asleep because your brain doesn't stop thinking?

Doctors recommend that teens get eight to ten hours of sleep each night. Adding mindfulness to your bedtime routine might help you clear your mind and get a better night's sleep. Follow these tips:

- If you can finish homework early, choose relaxing evening activities before bed, such as reading a book, playing a board game or cards, or talking with family or friends.
- Avoid drinking caffeinated drinks (such as soda or coffee) or high-sugar foods (such as chocolate) in the afternoon and evening. Caffeine is likely to keep you awake. Chocolate also has caffeine, and a diet of too much sugar can contribute to depression.

- Avoid looking at your smartphone or laptop an hour or two before bedtime. The blue light emitted by devices can disturb sleep.
- Dim the lights around you an hour before bedtime. Bright light suppresses the secretion of melatonin, a hormone that influences sleepiness.
- Cool the room where you sleep, if you can, by turning down the thermostat or opening a window a little bit to let in fresh air.
- Take a warm shower or bath an hour before bed. Then step out into a cooler room. The drop in body temperature will prepare you for sleep.
- Make your bedroom as dark as possible. For example, be sure to close the drapes or blinds. If you have lightweight window coverings, try a heavier fabric or shade to keep out more light. Or wear an eye mask.
- If you still can't fall asleep, get out of bed and do a quiet activity (avoiding screens) until you feel sleepy.

Try adding any of the following mindfulness exercises to your nighttime routine before you go to sleep. They might help you drift off.

## Alternate Nostril Breathing

Sit in a mindful posture.

Start by taking three mindful breaths.

Notice the expansion and contraction of your chest and belly as you breathe.

Relax more and more with each breath.

Imagine sinking deeply into your seat.

With your right palm open, fold down your index, middle, and ring fingers.

Block your right nostril with your right thumb.

Inhale slowly through your left nostril, and hold your breath for the count of four.

Release your right nostril, and block your left nostril with your right pinkie finger.

Exhale through your right nostril and inhale again.

Hold your breath for the count of four.

Block your right nostril again.

Exhale through your left nostril, and inhale again.

Continue for five more rounds.

## Mind Clearing

Lie down wherever you want to sleep.

Adjust a pillow under your head to make your shoulders, neck, and head comfortable.

Adjust your body position until you are comfortable, with your arms by your side.


Notice the thoughts in your mind.

Acknowledge these thoughts without judgment.

Imagine your thoughts as gray smoke inside you.


Imagine a glowing ball of white light hanging just above your head.

Give this light the power of kindness and compassion.

See the white light expand and stream down into your head and body.

As the white light fills you, it pushes the gray smoke out of your nose, mouth, and ears.

The gray smoke of your thoughts vanishes into the air.


Let your mind focus on the white light streaming down into you.

Imagine the freshness it brings.

Imagine it clearing away all of your thoughts, to let you rest deeply.

Relax into the steady rhythm of your breathing.

Your day is done.

## Four-Seven-Eight Breathing

Lie down wherever you want to sleep.

Adjust a pillow under your head to make your shoulders, neck, and head comfortable.

Adjust your body position until you are comfortable, with your arms by your side.

Touch the tip of your tongue to the roof of your mouth behind your front teeth.

Breathe in quietly through your nose to the count of four.

Hold your breath to the count of seven.

Breathe out of your mouth with a soft whooshing sound to the count of eight.

Repeat this process as long as you like.

# 8
# HAPPINESS:
# A MINDFUL WAY OF LIVING

Matthieu Ricard, the French scientist turned Buddhist monk who's famous for being happy, believes that anyone can use mindfulness to achieve happiness. But what is happiness and how can mindfulness point us toward it?

Many people believe that having money, fame, or success will make them happy. According to research, such circumstances can contribute to happiness. Yet people who have all that may still feel unhappy.

If you look up *happiness* in *Merriam-Webster's Collegiate Dictionary*, you'll see that the first definition of the word is "a state of well-being or contentment." The second definition is "a pleasurable or satisfying experience." So is happiness a state of mind or an experience?

Actually, it's both. Neuroscientists and psychologists who study happiness say that about 50 percent of a person's happiness comes from

There is no one formula for happiness, but studies show that doing meaningful activities, making strong personal connections, and accomplishing goals can all contribute to a sense of well-being.

genetic brain chemistry, something you were born with. The brain chemicals serotonin, dopamine, oxytocin, and endorphins assist in keeping people emotionally balanced and happy. Does that mean you're stuck with the level of happiness you feel now because of your genes?

The answer is no. Environment and experiences also play a major role in happiness. Scientists say that besides the 50 percent genetic contribution, 10 percent of happiness is due to external circumstances, such as having enough food, a safe home, and enough money to pay your bills. That leaves 40 percent of a person's happiness under their control. So you can contribute to your own happiness through attitudes and actions. That's where mindfulness comes in. A mindfulness practice can help you become aware of your attitudes and inspire positive actions.

## NO SINGLE FORMULA FOR HAPPINESS

Happiness is different for everyone. One person's path to happiness may not look like another's. But for most people, happiness includes both good feelings and positive experiences. Those experiences might include having strong friendships, volunteering in the community, playing on a sports team, or acting in a school play. Happiness involves taking part in activities that are meaningful to us, making connections to people we care about, and accomplishing goals we set for ourselves.

Happiness can also come from difficulties and challenges. How is that possible? By handling challenges with a positive outlook, a person can transform pain and suffering into something meaningful. Going through tough times might make you temporarily unhappy, but it might also make you wiser and more compassionate to those who experience similar difficulties. And the qualities of wisdom and compassion will contribute to your sense of purpose, well-being, and connection to other people.

# PRIMING THE BODY FOR HAPPINESS

You can affect your own level of happiness by putting your body, mind, and heart into becoming happier. When you wake up each morning, consider how you can add "happiness ingredients" to your day. Here are some ideas to get started:

**Exercise.** Exercise is at the top of the list of happiness ingredients. It can trigger a release of brain chemicals—including norepinephrine, serotonin, and dopamine—that are associated with mood, self-confidence, and enhanced well-being. Even walking just thirty minutes a day can reduce feelings of depression. So hop on a bike, walk with a friend, or take up a sport. Yoga and tai chi—both forms of movement that focus on connecting the breath and body—are good choices for adding mindfulness to your movement.

**Sunshine.** Exposure to bright light, especially sunshine, is essential for the body's release of serotonin. When serotonin levels are too low, you may feel irritable, anxious, and unsociable. Sunshine also triggers our bodies to produce vitamin D. A lack of this vitamin can cause fatigue, muscle aches, and depression. So crawl out of your cave and soak up

some sun. Don't forget to protect your skin from sun damage by wearing a hat and sunscreen if you will be exposed to the sun for long.

**Nature.** Being in nature has been shown to reduce anxiety and distress and to increase attention and awareness. A 2015 study at Stanford University in California showed that people who took a nature walk showed decreased anxiety and rumination (overthinking) and improved memory. Scientists in Japan have conducted research on the benefits of walking in nature. In the early 1990s, staff at the Japanese Ministry of Agriculture, Forestry and Fisheries coined the term *shinrin-yoku*, which means "forest bathing." *Forest bathing* means "taking a walk in the woods, using all your senses as you immerse yourself in nature." Philip Barr, a physician of integrative medicine at Duke University in North Carolina, says, "Medical researchers in Japan have studied forest bathing and have demonstrated several benefits to our health." In one study comparing walkers in the city and forest walkers, scientists found that those who walked in the forest had greater reductions in blood pressure and stress hormone.

So why not take a walk in the woods or in a park? If you live in an urban area, organize an outing to a nearby nature area. Or take

Research has shown that connecting with the natural world can have a calming effect. Some doctors prescribe spending time outdoors as a treatment for depression and anxiety.

a mindful walk, without looking at your phone, down a tree-lined street. If you cannot find a way to be in nature, try meditating on a photo of a nature setting. Studies show this may have a similar effect to being in nature.

**Eating for nutrients.** If you want to eat for happiness, mindfully choose foods that boost your vitamin count and promote physical and mental health. Think colorful fruits and veggies. Researchers have found that complex carbohydrates, in foods such as oatmeal, brown rice, and whole-grain bread, promote the release of serotonin. Substances called omega-3 fatty acids boost mood, concentration, and energy and help reduce anxiety and depression. You can add them to your diet by eating fatty fish—salmon and tuna—as well as eggs. Eggs also contain vitamin D, which helps your mood. If you eat a cafeteria lunch at school, talk to the school's cafeteria manager about adding more fresh fruits and vegetables, complex carbohydrates, and omega-3 fatty acids to the menu. And if you live far from a fresh food market, think about growing a vegetable garden in your yard or on the patio. Some neighborhoods have community gardens, where individuals each get space to grow their own plants.

**Sleep.** Sleep is essential to happiness. When you don't get enough sleep, you are more likely to feel depressed, overreact to stressful situations, and think less clearly. Some signs that you need more sleep are feeling sad for no obvious reason, being forgetful or foggy-brained, being clumsy, or being irritable or grumpy. Experts say teens need eight to ten hours of sleep a night. Teen brains are still maturing, and they, therefore, need more time to repair, maintain their cells, and clear out toxic metabolites, small molecules produced as the body functions. Sleep deprivation can even damage your physical health. It can lead to increased abdominal fat and high blood pressure. It can also affect your concentration, memory, and blood sugar levels. Not sleeping enough is just no good for your health and happiness.

But what if you can't get to bed or fall asleep before 11 p.m. and have to wake up at 7 a.m. for school—and that's on a good day? Some school districts are making high school schedule changes so that teens don't have to start school so early. If that's not happening where you live, try to adapt your schedule so you can get more sleep during the week. Keeping regular sleep hours is best. If you can't get eight to ten hours per night during the week, adding extra hours on weekends and holidays might reduce the negative health effects of sleep deprivation, according to a 2018 study in the *Journal of Sleep Research*. If falling asleep is a problem for you, mindfulness meditation and breathing exercises might help you fall asleep with more ease.

# TURNING THE MIND TOWARD HAPPINESS

The mind is a powerful tool for happiness, and actions contribute too. Here are some more suggestions that could help you increase happiness:

**Meditation.** Meditation can trigger the release of "happy" brain chemicals. It can boost endorphin and serotonin levels, and reduce cortisol (stress hormone) levels, helping you feel calm and content. Start with short sessions, building up to longer sessions over time. Neuroscientists are still trying to determine how much meditation is needed for health benefits. They say that frequency and consistency are more important than the amount of time you meditate. So schedule meditation into each day. To make it a habit, try meditating at the same time every day.

**Gratitude.** Giving thanks and feeling grateful are strongly connected to happiness. Practicing gratitude is simple. Whenever you can, thank someone in person for their kindness or for being in your life. Take time to write about the things for which you are grateful. You could keep a gratitude journal. Or write short notes about what makes you feel grateful and keep them in a shoebox. Look at your notes occasionally, or add to them. You could also write a thank-you note and send it to someone who treated you well. You can meditate on gratitude too, thinking of the people and experiences for which you are grateful and that matter to you.

**Social engagement.** Having good friends and being socially engaged is one of the most reliable predictors of happiness and good health overall. And the quality of a friendship matters more than the quantity. Social engagements must feel like a good fit to add to happiness. Introverts might be happiest with one or two close friends instead of a big peer group, for example. Spend time figuring out what matters to you and how you can build friendships. Do you prefer a computer coding group, a cosplay meetup, a book club, a debating team, or a volunteer job at a local animal shelter? Maybe none of these ideas appeals to you, so take time to explore what type of social engagement will increase your happiness.

**Bypassing the negativity bias.** Humans have a negativity bias. We tend to obsess about the negative things in our lives and often forget the positive. Is that true for you? Think about a day when something

"Happiness is impermanent, like everything else. In order for happiness to be extended and renewed, you have to learn how to feed your happiness."

—Thich Nhat Hanh, Buddhist, spiritual leader and author

went wrong. Did your brain go over it again and again, or did you forget about it and focus on more positive aspects of your life? You can change this negativity bias with mindfulness practice. Whenever you are obsessing about the negative, choose to shift your attitude. Practice any mindfulness exercise you like, or take a mindful moment to practice this exercise for recalling a happy memory.

## Recall a Happy Memory

Take three mindful breaths.

Notice the expansion and contraction of your chest and belly as you breathe.

Relax more and more with each breath.

Imagine sinking deeply into your seat.

Recall a time when you were really happy. Close your eyes to go deeper into the memory.

What were you doing?

Concentrate on the details of this memory. Where were you, and who were you with? Maybe you were alone and enjoying the solitude. If you were outdoors, what season was it? Can you remember any good smells? What other feel-good sensations can you bring to mind?

Imagine telling someone about this good memory, reliving it as you do.

Let the good feelings of this memory wash over you.

Rest in this state for a few minutes before you carry on with your day.

The more often you do this practice, the more quickly your mind will get used to it and move toward the positive.

Self-compassion is also strongly associated with happiness and well-being. If you are feeling hypercritical of yourself, try to loosen up and treat yourself as you would your best friend. Try this exercise:

# Practice Self-Compassion

Take three mindful breaths.

Notice the expansion and contraction of your chest and belly as
    you breathe.

Relax more and more with each breath.

Imagine sinking deeply into your seat.

Imagine that a good friend comes to you with a problem. Perhaps they
feel bad about how they treated someone who asked them out on a date.
Or maybe they don't like the way they look or how they fit in their
clothes. How do you respond? In your mind, listen to the words you choose
to say and your tone of voice. Write down these words if you like.

Think about when you have felt bad about yourself. Maybe you treated a
friend in an unkind way. Maybe you did poorly on a test. Maybe you don't
like the way you look. Notice what you say to yourself and if your tone is
harsh. Jot down these words too.

Next, compare the words you used with the close friend to the ones you
used with yourself. Are you tougher on yourself? If so, in what way and
why? Does that extra toughness motivate you or make you feel stuck
and depressed?

Imagine your best friend encouraging you in the same way you would
encourage them. Talk to yourself in the same positive voice. Tell yourself
it's okay not to be perfect. It's also great to discover your own style and
way of being. Remind yourself that people love and admire you for who
you are—your humor, your kindness, and your sense of fun—and not for
how you look. Write down positive, compassionate statements to reaffirm
them in your mind.

Remind yourself that you are wonderful and that you matter just as
you are. Any time your critical voice comes into your mind, respond to it
with compassion.

# ACTS OF KINDNESS

Some people think that being kind to others benefits only the receiver and that the giver shouldn't expect and doesn't get anything in return. But the opposite is true. Practicing kindness and compassion can boost your own happiness and aid your physical well-being. Sonja Lyubomirsky, professor of psychology at the University of California–Riverside, focuses much of her research on kindness, happiness, and their health benefits. Her studies have shown that doing good for others can increase the giver's positive emotions and decrease negative emotions.

Does that mean that helping others is selfish? Not according to the Dalai Lama, a famous Tibetan Buddhist monk, teacher, and author who won the 1989 Nobel Peace Prize and many humanitarian awards for his compassionate work. He calls kind behavior "wise-selfish." He means that our own personal happiness is tied to that of others. Human beings are interdependent, so helping others can give us a sense of purpose, which is an integral part of happiness.

So go ahead and practice kindness. You could do something kind for a sibling or friend. Or organize a food drive for a local homeless shelter. You could form a team and pick up trash along sidewalks near your school or home. Or rake leaves, mow the lawn, or shovel snow for an elderly neighbor who might need help. It can be something even simpler, such as saying "thank you" or "great idea" more often. Or letting someone else go first or holding the door for a stranger.

"Each of us has a responsibility for all humankind . . . if you try to subdue your selfish motives–anger, and so forth–and develop more kindness and compassion for others, ultimately you yourself will benefit more than you would otherwise. . . . Foolish selfish people are always thinking of themselves, and the result is negative. Wise selfish people think of others, help others as much as they can, and the result is that they too receive benefit."

—Dalai Lama, Nobel Peace Prize laureate and author

There's no end to opportunities to be kind if you turn your mind in that direction. You can enhance the experience of kindness with this loving-kindness meditation. To make it effective, direct your loving-kindness first toward yourself and then toward others.

## Loving-Kindness Meditation

Sit in a mindful posture. Take three mindful breaths.
Notice the expansion and contraction of your chest and belly as
    you breathe.
Relax more and more with each breath.
Imagine sinking deeply into your seat.

Think of someone who makes you feel happy and loved.
Focus on the feelings of kindness in your heart when you visualize
    this person.
See that warmth as golden rays of light shining in your heart and
    surrounding you.

Imagine sending your golden light to someone you love, perhaps a close
    friend or family member.
Imagine your light streaming into the heart of that person, making
    them happy.

Send your golden light of kindness to someone you don't know well or
    even someone who makes you feel grumpy.
Let the light sink into that person. Imagine that person becoming happy.

Finally, share your golden light with everyone in the world.
Imagine you can ease suffering with your kindness.
Rest in a shared feeling of compassion for a few moments.

Repeat to yourself, "May I and all others be happy, healthy, and safe."
Take three more soft, slow mindful breaths before you finish
    your meditation.

Many spiritual leaders, such as the Dalai Lama, teach that we can increase our own happiness by helping others.

# INTENTION

Mindfulness, as a way of being, is a method for opening up to yourself and patiently expanding your awareness of the present moment. You can strengthen your mindfulness practice each day by adding a mindful intention. Remember, intentions are not the same as goals. Intentions are sources of inspiration that help us shape our attitudes as we move through our day.

Choose an intention for your day. The list on the opposite page can get you started. Check in with yourself during the day to see if you are holding onto your intention. At the end of each day, reflect on how that intention influenced you. If you forget to think of your intention during the day, don't worry. The moment you notice that you've forgotten your intention is a moment of mindfulness.

"Engaging in particular intentional activities is the most effective method of boosting chronic happiness."

—Sonja Lyubomirsky, psychology professor, and Matthew D. Della Porta, consultant

# INTENTIONS

| | |
|---|---|
| acceptance | love |
| calm | nonjudgment |
| compassion | open-mindedness |
| forgiveness | patience |
| friendliness | peacefulness |
| generosity | respect |
| gratefulness | self-acceptance |
| helpfulness | tolerance |
| honesty | trust |
| kindness | understanding |

## DEDICATING THE MERIT

One last element of mindfulness involves dedicating the merit or positive effects of your practice to someone else. This is a way of turning your mind toward others. When you do this, you are saying to yourself, "If I benefit from mindfulness, I extend the positive outcome that I receive and share it with others." Through mindfulness, you may become a happier, wiser, and more compassionate being, so you benefit—and the people around you benefit too.

We all have hard times. We all have difficult emotions and troubling thoughts. What we might forget when we are going through challenges is that we can control how we experience and react to them. When we choose mindfulness, we are opening our hearts to happiness and looking for the calm within.

# SOURCE NOTES

6   Mat Smith, "How to Be Happy (According to the World's Happiest Man),"
    *Esquire*, January 18, 2015, https://www.esquire.com/uk/life/fitness-wellbeing
    /news/a4915/matthieu-ricard-what-ive-learned/.

6   Kashmira Gander, "The World's Happiest Man Reveals What Makes Him
    Unhappy," *Independent* (London), October 17, 2016, https://www.independent
    .co.uk/life-style/health-and-families/matthieu-ricard-worlds-happiest-man
    -unhappy-buddhist-nepal-book-photographer-a7365191.html.

6   Smith, "How to Be Happy."

8   Antoine Lutz et al, "Long-Term Meditators Self-Induce High Amplitude Gamma
    Synchrony during Mental Practice," *Proceedings of the National Academy of
    Sciences*, November 16, 2004, http://www.pnas.org/content/101/46/16369.short.

8   "Mind Fitness: How Meditation Boosts Your Focus, Resilience, and Brain,"
    YouTube video, 7:24, posted by Big Think, January 13, 2018, https://www
    .youtube.com/watch?v=ybSZk7RhO1A.

8   Smith, "How to Be Happy."

13  B. J. Gallagher, "Buddha: How to Tame Your Monkey Mind," Huffington Post,
    September 3, 2011, https://www.huffingtonpost.com/bj-gallagher/buddha-how
    -to-tame-your-m_b_945793.html.

13  Padmasambhava, *Dzogchen Essentials: The Path That Clarifies Confusion*
    (Boulder, CO: Rangjung Yeshe, 2004), 278.

13  Arbo Laibowitz, "Jon Kabat-Zinn, the Father of Mindfulness and MBSR,"
    Happiness.org, accessed October 3, 2018, https://www.happiness.org/jon-kabat
    -zinn/.

25  Lama Lena, teaching at Tibetan House in New Orleans, January 12, 2018.

33  Eckhart Tolle, *The Power of Now* (Vancouver, BC: Namaste/New World Library,
    1999), 17.

43  Lisa Feldman Barrett. "You Aren't at the Mercy of Your Emotions. Your Brain
    Creates Them." TED, December 2017, https://www.ted.com/talks/lisa_
    feldman_barrett_you_aren_t_at_the_mercy_of_your_emotions_your_brain_
    creates_them#t-677082.

46  Grace P., interview with author at Patrick Taylor Science and Technology
    Academy, Westwego, LA, May 2, 2018.

50  Balseba T., interview with author at Patrick Taylor Science and Technology
    Academy, Westwego, LA, May 2, 2018.

50  Grace P., interview.

53  Grace P.

53 Artemis, interview with author at Patrick Taylor Science and Technology Academy, Westwego, LA, May 2, 2018.

53 Balseba T., interview.

56 Adam Avin, Facetime interview with author, May 23, 2018.

56 Mae H., interview with author at Patrick Taylor Science and Technology Academy, Westwego, LA, May 3, 2018.

57 E. Parnell, interview with author at Patrick Taylor Science and Technology Academy, Westwego, LA, May 2, 2018.

68 Jean M. Twenge, "Have Smartphones Destroyed a Generation?," *Atlantic*, September 2017, https://www.theatlantic.com/magazine/archive/2017/09/has-the -smartphone-destroyed-a-generation/534198/.

68 Beatrice E., Facetime interview with author, April 18, 2018.

68 Balseba T., interview with author at Patrick Taylor Science and Technology Academy Westwego, LA, May 3, 2018.

68 E. Parnell, interview.

68 Dominic C., Facebook interview with author, May 30, 2018.

69 Twenge, "Smartphones."

72 Maggie S., Facetime interview with author, May 6, 2018.

72 Elizabeth Grace, interview with author at Patrick Taylor Science and Technology Academy, Westwego, LA, May 3, 2018.

72 Beatrice E., interview.

72 Alexander B., Facetime interview with author, April 26, 2018.

87 Maggie S., interview.

93 *Meriam-Webster's Collegiate Dictionary*, 10th ed. (Springfield, MA: Meriam-Webster 1998), 528.

96 Allison Aubrey, "Forest Bathing: A Retreat to Nature Can Boost Immunity and Mood," *NPR, Morning Edition*, July 17, 2017, https://www.npr.org/sections /health-shots/2017/07/17/536676954/forest-bathing-a-retreat-to-nature-can -boost-immunity-and-mood\.

99 Thich Nhat Hanh, "5 Practices for Nurturing Happiness," *Lion's Roar*, March 27, 2017, https://www.lionsroar.com/5-practices-for-nurturing-happiness/.

102 Aubrey, "Forest Bathing."

102 Dalai Lama, *A Policy of Kindness* (Ithaca, NY: Snow Lion, 1990), 52.

104 Sonja Lyubomirsky and Matthew D. Della Porta, "Boosting Happiness, Buttressing Resilience: Results from Cognitive Behavioral Interventions," SonjaLyubomirsky.com, accessed October 3, 2018, http://sonjalyubomirsky .com/wp-content/themes/sonjalyubomirsky/papers/LDinpressb.pdf.

# GLOSSARY

**adrenaline:** another name for epinephrine, a hormone secreted by the adrenal glands. Epinephrine causes changes in the body, such as increased heart rate and increased blood pressure.

**amygdala:** a structure in the brain that controls response to emotions, especially fear. The body's fight-or-flight response begins in the amygdala.

**anxiety:** a common emotion, marked by feelings of fear, dread, or nervousness

**Buddhism:** a religion founded by Siddhartha Gautama in India around 500 BCE. Mindfulness meditation has its roots in Buddhism.

**compassion:** understanding the feelings of others and wanting to help

**constructed sense of self:** the idea of oneself that comes from defining who you are with thoughts and labels

**cortisol:** a hormone secreted by the adrenal glands in response to stress. Cortisol helps convert glycogen into glucose, a sugar that fuels the body.

**depression:** a mental disorder marked by long periods of sadness, hopelessness, despondency, and other negative thoughts and emotions

**epinephrine:** also called adrenaline, a hormone secreted by the adrenal glands. Epinephrine causes changes in the body, such as increased heart rate and increased blood pressure.

**eustress:** a positive form of stress, with a beneficial effect on health, motivation, performance, and emotional well-being. Eustress can accompany a challenging, exciting, or intense physical experience, such as playing sports.

**fight-or-flight response:** the body's reaction to a stressful or dangerous situation. During this response, the body undergoes changes, such as increased heart rate and blood pressure. These changes prepare the body to fight off a threat or to flee from it. Over time, excessive activation of the fight-or-flight response can have harmful effects on physical and emotional health.

**guided meditation:** a session in which meditators follow a series of prompts from a teacher or leader, either in person or through a recording or written text

**hormone:** a chemical substance that controls a body activity, such as growth or reproduction. In stressful situations, the body releases stress hormones such as epinephrine and cortisol.

**insomnia:** the inability to fall asleep or to stay asleep

**meditation:** a mental discipline or practice of staying focused and alert, and resting the mind in a calm, relaxed, and natural state of awareness

**mindfulness:** a way of being or a practice of paying attention, on purpose and with patience, to inner and outer experiences, without judgment

**monkey mind:** endless chatter in the mind that can distract present-moment awareness

**negativity bias:** the human tendency to focus on negative events or experiences more than positive ones

**serotonin:** a brain chemical that contributes to a sense of well-being and happiness

**yoga:** a mental and physical practice based on Hindu teachings

# SELECTED BIBLIOGRAPHY

Anderson, Jenny. "New Research Shows One Kind of Teenage Friendship Is More Likely to Result in a Happier, Healthy Adulthood." Quartz, August 23, 2017. https://qz.com/1059666/having-a-stronger-closer-friendship-as-a-teenager-predicts-less-depression-as-a-young-adult/.

Baer, Ruth, and Willem Kuyken. "Is Mindfulness Safe." *Mindful*, May 23, 2016. https://www.mindful.org/is-mindfulness-safe/.

Bergland, Christoper. "Mindfulness Mediation and the Vagus Nerve Share Many Powers." *Psychology Today*, February 5, 2016. https://www.psychologytoday.com/us/blog/the-athletes-way/201602/mindfulness-meditation-and-the-vagus-nerve-share-many-powers.

———. "The Neurochemicals of Happiness." *Psychology Today*, November 29, 2012. https://www.psychologytoday.com/us/blog/the-athletes-way/201211/the-neurochemicals-happiness.

Berman, Marc G., Ethan Kross, Katherine M. Krpan, Mary Askren, Aleah Burson, Patricia J. Deldin, Stephen Kaplan et al. "Interacting with Nature Improves Cognition and Affect for Individuals with Depression." *Journal of Affective Disorders* 140, no. 3 (November 2012): 300–305. https://web.stanford.edu/group/mood/cgi-bin/wordpress/wp-content/uploads/2012/08/Berman-JAD-2012.pdf.

Britton, Alexander. "Instagram and Snapchat Are Damaging Young People's Mental Health, Study Warns." *Mirror* (London), May 19, 2017. https://www.mirror.co.uk/tech/instagram-snapchat-harming-young-peoples-10453593.

Buchanan, Kathryn E., and Anat Bardi. "Acts of Kindness and Acts of Novelty Affect Life Satisfaction." *Journal of Social Psychology* 150, no. 3 (April 2010): 235–237. https://www.researchgate.net/publication/44797453_Acts_of_Kindness_and_Acts_of_Novelty_Affect_Life_Satisfaction.

Campbell, Leigh. "'Compassion Meditation' Is the Best Type to Practice If Happiness Is Your Goal." Huffington Post. Last modified February 14, 2017. https://www.huffingtonpost.com.au/2017/02/12/compassion-meditation-is-the-best-type-to-practise-if-happines_a_21712408/.

Crum, A. J., P. Salovey, and S. Achor. "Rethinking Stress: The Role of Mindsets in Determining the Stress Response." *Journal of Personality and Social Psychology* 104, no. 4 (April 2013): 716–733.

Cuda, Gretchen. "Just Breathe: Body Has a Built-In Stress Reliever." *NPR*, December 6, 2010. https://www.npr.org/2010/12/06/131734718/just-breathe-body-has-a-built-in-stress-reliever.

Fox, Kara. "Instagram Worst Social Media App for Young People's Mental Health." *CNN*, May 19, 2017. https://www.cnn.com/2017/05/19/health/instagram-worst-social-network-app-young-people-mental-health/index.html.

Friedman, Richard. "The Stress Sweet Spot." *New York Times,* June 1, 2018.

Garcia, Silvia. "40% Happiness Depends on Our Decisions." Thrive Global, November 13, 2017. https://www.thriveglobal.com/stories/15893-40-happiness -depends-on-our-decisions.

"Giving Thanks Can Make You Happier." Harvard Health Publishing. Accessed December 18, 2018. https://www.health.harvard.edu/healthbeat/giving-thanks-can -make-you-happier.

Goleman, Daniel. "Mind Fitness: How Meditation Boosts Your Focus, Resilience, and Brain." YouTube video, 7:24. Posted by Big Think, January 13, 2018. https:// www.youtube.com/watch?v=ybSZk7RhO1A.

Goleman, Daniel, and Richard Davidson. *Altered Traits: Science Reveals How Meditation Changes You Mind, Brain, and Body.* New York: Avery, 2017.

Heffernan, Virginia. "The Muddled Meaning of 'Mindfulness.'" *New York Times*, April 14, 2015.

Holmes, Lindsay. "All the Ways Sleep Affects Your Happiness, in One Chart." Huffington Post, July 23, 2015. https://www.huffingtonpost.com/entry/all-the-ways -sleep-affects-your-happiness-in-one-char_us_55ae4d55e4b07af29d564a29.

Ireland, Tom. "What Does Mindfulness Meditation Do to Your Brain?" *Scientific American*, June 12, 2014. https://blogs.scientificamerican.com/guest-blog/what-does -mindfulness-meditation-do-to-your-brain/.

LeDoux, Joseph E., "The Amygdala Is NOT the Brain's Fear Center." *Psychology Today*, August 10, 2015. https://www.psychologytoday.com/us/blog/i-got-mind-tell -you/201508/the-amygdala-is-not-the-brains-fear-center.

Lenhart, Amanda. "Teens, Technology and Friendships." Pew Research Center, August 6, 2015. http://www.pewinternet.org/2015/08/06/teens-technology-and -friendships/.

Lyubomirsky, Sonja. *The Myths of Happiness: What Should Make You Happy but Doesn't, What Shouldn't Make You Happy but Does.* New York: Penguin, 2013.

McGreevey, Sue. "Turn Down the Volume." *Harvard Gazette*, April 22, 2011. https:// news.harvard.edu/gazette/story/2011/04/turn-down-the-volume/.

"More Sleep Would Make Us Happier, Healthier and Safer." American Psychological Association, February 2014. http://www.apa.org/action/resources/research-in-action /sleep-deprivation.aspx.

Morris, David Z. "Less Work, Less Sex, Less Happiness: We're Losing Generation Z to the Smartphone." *Fortune,* August 6, 2017. http://fortune.com/2017/08/06 /generation-z-smartphone-depression/.

———. "Social Media Is Fueling a Scary Trend for Teen Anxiety." *Fortune*, October 15, 2017. http://fortune.com/2017/10/15/social-media-teen-anxiety/.

Odgers, Candice. "It's Easy to Blame Smartphones for Teens' Mental Health Issues. But It's Wrong." *Fortune*, April 6, 2018. http://fortune.com/2018/04/06/teens-youths -mental-health-smartphones-addicted/.

"Pay Attention: Exploring How Forest Bathing Benefits Both Body and Mind." *CBS This Morning*, June 8, 2018. https://www.cbsnews.com/news/pay-attention-forest -bathing-therapy-effect-on-our-bodies-and-brains/.

"Pay Attention: Finding Balance in the Age of Tech." *CBS This Morning*, March 14, 2018. https://www.cbsnews.com/news/pay-attention-finding-balance-technology/.

Powell, Alvin. "When Science Meets Mindfulness." *Harvard Gazette*, April 9, 2018. https://news.harvard.edu/gazette/story/2018/04/harvard-researchers-study-how -mindfulness-may-change-the-brain-in-depressed-patients/.

Reynolds, Gretchen. "To Train an Athlete, Add 12 Minutes of Meditation to the Daily Mix." *New York Times*, June 21, 2017.

Siegel, Daniel. "The Science of Mindfulness." *Mindful*, September 7, 2010. https:// www.mindful.org/the-science-of-mindfulness/.

Van Damm, Nicholas T., M. K. van Vugt, D. R. Vago, L. Schmalzl, C. D. Saron, A. Olendzki, T. Meissner et al. "Mind the Hype: A Critical Evaluation and Prescriptive Agenda for Research on Mindfulness and Meditation." *Perspectives on Psychological Science* 13, no. 1 (January 2018): 36–61.

Walton, Alice G. "Science Shows Meditation Benefits Children's Brains and Behavior." *Forbes*, October 18, 2016. https://www.forbes.com/sites/alicegwalton /2016/10/18/the-many-benefits-of-meditation-for-children/#50b8bf7bdbe3.

"What Is the Science of Happiness?" Berkeley Wellness, November 9, 2015. http:// www.berkeleywellness.com/healthy-mind/mind-body/article/what-science-happiness.

Wright, Robert. "Is Mindfulness Meditation a Capitalist Tool or a Path to Enlightenment? Yes." Wired, October 12, 2017. https://www.wired.com/2017/08/the -science-and-philosophy-of-mindfulness-meditation/.

# FURTHER INFORMATION

## Books

Biegel, Gina. *Be Mindful: Card Deck for Teens*. Eau Claire, WI: Pesi, 2016.

Biegel, Gina, and Todd H. Corbin. *Mindfulness for Student Athletes: A Workbook to Help Teens Reduce Stress and Enhance Performance*. Oakland: Instant Help Books, 2018.

Dalai Lama and Howard Cutler. *The Art of Happiness in a Troubled World*. New York: Harmony Books, 2009.

Dalai Lama and Paul Ekman. *Emotional Awareness: Overcoming the Obstacles to Psychological Balance and Compassion*. New York: Holt, 2009.

Goldstein, Joseph. *Mindfulness: A Practical Guide to Awakening*. Louisville, CO: Sounds True, 2016.

Harris, Dan, Jeffrey Warren, and Carlyle Adler. *Meditation for Fidgety Skeptics: A 10% Happier How-to Book*. New York: Spiegel & Grau, 2017.

Kabat-Zinn, Jon. *Full Catastrophe Living: Using the Wisdom of Your Body and Mind to Face Stress, Pain, and Illness*. New York: Bantam Books, 2013.

McGraw, Sally. *Living Simply: A Teen Guide to Minimalism*. Minneapolis: Twenty-First Century Books, 2019.

Salzberg, Sharon. *Real Happiness: The Power of Meditation*. New York: Workman, 2011.

Vo, Dzung X. *The Mindful Teen: Powerful Skills to Help You Handle Stress One Moment at a Time*. Oakland: Instant Help Books, 2015.

# Websites

Atlas of Emotions
> http://atlasofemotions.org/
> This is an excellent interactive tool for exploring your emotional world. It helps you gain control over what triggers your emotions and how you respond. It's also fun!

Center for Healthy Minds
> https://centerhealthyminds.org/
> What if the world were a kinder, wiser, and more compassionate place? This is the central question posed by this center at the University of Wisconsin–Madison. This is a great site to read about cool research on the mind, the brain, and emotion.

Center for Mindfulness in Medicine, Health Care, and Society
> https://www.umassmed.edu/cfm/
> This site offers online courses in mindfulness-based stress reduction and mindfulness-based cognitive therapy for depression. It's also a great source for research articles.

Greater Good Magazine
> https://greatergood.berkeley.edu/
> This site has videos, quizzes, and podcasts on science-based insights for a meaningful life. Test your emotional intelligence to see how well you read other people.

Kids Association for Mindfulness in Education
> http://www.mindfuleducation.org/kame/
> Teenager Adam Avin created the Kids Association for Mindfulness in Education so that tweens and teens can share their voices about current events and mindfully make this world a better place. Avin also created Wuf Shanti, a yoga and wellness program for younger children.

Life's Good—Experience Happiness
> http://www.lg.com/us/experiencehappiness
> This site links readers with simple principles of happiness and with research articles on happiness.

Mindful
> https://www.mindful.org/
> This is a great resource for articles about mindfulness and everyday life. Check out the sections "Love & Relationships" and "Body & Mind."

Mindfulness for Teens
> http://mindfulnessforteens.com/guided-meditations/
> This site, hosted by pediatrician and mindfulness author Dr. Dzung Vo, includes recordings of mindfulness exercises.

Mindsight Institute

https://www.mindsightinstitute.com/

Dr. Daniel Siegel, a clinical professor of psychology, is the founder of Mindsight Institute, which offers online lectures and courses for students, educators, parents, health-care professionals, and the general public.

Stressed Teens

https://www.stressedteens.com/

Psychologist and mindfulness instructor Gina Biegel offers online mindfulness-based stress reduction courses for teens and teacher-training courses for parents and professionals.

Tara Brach

https://www.tarabrach.com/

Tara Brach is a psychologist and a meditation teacher with a compassionate heart. She has guided meditations and public talks that are both soothing and inspiring.

## Mindfulness and Meditation Apps

Calm

https://www.calm.com/

Calm is currently the number one app for meditation and sleep. Sessions focus on four areas: meditation, breathing, sleep, and relaxation. The meditation section offers a wide range of sessions, including managing stress, forgiveness, breaking habits, loving-kindness, and walking meditation. The sleep section includes meditations and bedtime stories to relax you at night. Calm also offers a master class in mindful eating. A free trial is available.

Headspace

https://www.headspace.com/

This app, which offers meditation sessions for sleep, stress, and more, is popular with young adults. The animated graphics make learning meditation fun. Headspace is also involved in the science of meditation and is working with the health-care industry to push for insurance coverage for meditation. A free trial is available.

Insight Timer

https://insighttimer.com/

The free app Insight Timer offers more than nine thousand guided meditations from a variety of well-known teachers, including Jack Kornfield and Sharon Salzberg. You'll find meditations in seven categories of practices: mindfulness, visualization, gentle repetition, movement, sound, concentration, and self-observation.

The Mindfulness App

http://themindfulnessapp.com/

This mindfulness app includes a five-day guided introduction to mindfulness and reminders to relax. This app has a library to suit all levels of mindfulness practitioners—from beginners to experts. It offers guided and silent timed sessions from three to thirty minutes. A free trial is available.

Stop, Breathe, & Think

https://www.stopbreathethink.com/

Stop, Breathe, & Think offers meditations on mindful breathing, body scan, kindness, gratitude, compassion, dealing with anxiety, and more. They vary from two to twenty minutes long. One called nature sounds is very relaxing if you prefer to meditate without listening to a guiding voice. A free trial is available.

# INDEX

# PHOTO ACKNOWLEDGMENTS

Image credits: Design: aaltair/Shutterstock.com (letters); Peratek/Shutterstock.com (clouds); Shtonado/Shutterstock.com (stones). Content: Moxie Productions/Blend Images/Getty Images, p. 7; World History Archive/Alamy Stock Photo, p. 9; D Dipasupil/Getty Images, p. 11; Laura Westlund/Independent Picture Service, pp. 16, 21, 23, 27, 55; skynesher/E+/Getty Images, p. 18; Hill Street Studios LLC/Getty Images, p. 31; Image Source/Getty Images, p. 38; JUAN GARTNER/Getty Images, p. 43; Jim Lane/Alamy Stock Photo, p. 54; nemke/Getty Images, p. 67; Stígur Már Karlsson/Heimsmyndir/Getty Images, p. 74; Hill Street Studios/Blend Images/Getty Images, p. 77; Fuse/Getty Images, p. 83; iStockphoto/Getty Images, p. 89; Hero Images/Getty Images, p. 94; Caiaimage/Trevor Adeline/Getty Images, pp. 96, 97; Alison Wright/Science Source/Getty Images, p. 104.

Cover: aaltair/Shutterstock.com (letters); Peratek/Shutterstock.com (clouds); Shtonado/Shutterstock.com (stones).

## ABOUT THE AUTHOR

Whitney Stewart graduated from Brown University and began writing children's books after traveling to Tibet in 1986 and interviewing the Dalai Lama in India for a biography for young readers. Since then she has continued to publish award-winning children's books while also studying and practicing mindfulness. Her most recent publications include *Mindful Kids: 50 Mindfulness Activities for Kindness, Focus, and Calm* (2017); *Mindful Me: Mindfulness for Kids* (2018); and *What's on Your Plate? Exploring the World of Food* (2018). To learn more about her work or contact her, go to www.whitneystewart.com.